Subject Matter Jurisdiction
Civil Procedure
Law Under the Scalpel: Case Dissections
(Law in Pieces)

Anjanette G. Seymour, LL.M., LL.B. (Hons.)

This work is published as part of the *Law in Pieces* series of study snippets. It is intended as an educational aid and should not be construed as a full textbook or novel. Nothing in this volume constitutes legal advice, nor does it create an attorney–client relationship. Readers should consult authoritative sources, case law, and qualified legal instructors for comprehensive guidance.

This book explains judicial opinions and legal doctrine in clear, original language. All case names and quotations from judicial opinions are in the public domain. The anatomical framework, narrative explanations, summaries, diagrams, and pedagogical structure are original works created by the author. Any errors or interpretations are the author's own.

Cover Design: Anjanette G. Seymour

ISBN: 9798995892335

TABLE OF CONTENTS

Civil Procedure: Subject-Matter Jurisdiction — Law Under the Scalpel: Case Dissections

Law in Pieces Series

6. Merrell Dow Pharmaceuticals v. Thompson (1986) — No Federal Cause of Action → No §1331
7. Grable & Sons v. Darue (2005) — Embedded Federal Issue Test
8. Gunn v. Minton (2013) — Substantiality Refinement

Part III — Diversity Jurisdiction

(Citizenship, domicile, amount, and timing)

9. St. Paul Mercury Indemnity Co. v. Red Cab Co. (1938) — Amount in Controversy
10. Mas v. Perry (1974) — Citizenship & Domicile
11. Grupo Dataflux v. Atlas Global Group (2004) — Time-of-Filing Rule
12. Hertz Corp. v. Friend (2010) — Nerve Center Test

Part IV — Supplemental Jurisdiction

(From common nucleus → collapse → revival)

13. United Mine Workers v. Gibbs (1966) — Common Nucleus Test
14. Finley v. United States (1989) — No Pendent-Party Jurisdiction
15. Exxon Mobil v. Allapattah Services (2005) — Supplemental Jurisdiction Over Additional Plaintiffs

Part V — Removal Jurisdiction

(Who may remove, when, and what defects matter)

16. Shamrock Oil & Gas Corp. v. Sheets (1941) — Only

Part VI — The Final Anatomy

Dedication

To every reader who reaches for clarity, courage, or simply a place to begin — this series is for you.
You who open these pages with curiosity, with hope, with the quiet belief that you can grow into the person you imagine. May these books meet you gently, guide you steadily, and remind you that understanding is not a gift — it is a journey. Thank you for letting my words walk beside you. Your presence on these pages is an honor, and your growth is the reason this work exists.

Epigraph

"Between doubt and destiny lies a single, steady truth: you are becoming someone extraordinary, one brave page at a time. Every journey begins with trembling hands — every triumph with a heart that refuses to quit."

— Anjanette G. Seymour

Series Preface

Law in Pieces: Under the Scalpel: Case Dissections

Law is often taught as if it were a fortress: towering, impenetrable, and guarded by centuries of doctrine. Students are told to scale its walls with outlines, mnemonics, and casebooks that speak in a language few understand on the first read. But law was never meant to be a fortress. It was meant to be a body — living, breathing, interconnected.

The Law in Pieces series was born from that belief.

Each volume in this series takes a major doctrinal area and places it under the scalpel. Not to destroy it, but to reveal its anatomy. To show the organs that keep it alive. To trace the arteries that carry meaning from one case to the next. To expose the fractures where courts struggle, innovate, or contradict themselves. And to give students the clarity that traditional materials too often obscure.

This is not a casebook. It is not a hornbook. It is a dissection.

Every case is treated as a patient. Every opinion is a surgical report. Every doctrine is a system of organs that must be understood in relation to the whole.

The goal is simple: Epiphany. Not memorization. Not regurgitation. But the moment when a student sees the structure beneath the surface and finally understands *why* the law works the way it does.

The first volume, Personal Jurisdiction, opened the body at the level of power over persons. This volume turns the scalpel toward Subject-Matter Jurisdiction, the power over cases themselves. Future volumes will continue the journey — each one a new organ system, each one a new opportunity to illuminate the law from the inside out.

This series is for the student who wants clarity. For the educator who wants a new way to teach. For the practitioner who wants to remember why the doctrine matters. And for the lifelong learner who believes that law, like the human body, is most beautiful when understood from within.

Welcome back to the operating room. Let us continue the dissection.

Author's Note

Law in Pieces began with memory.

I earned my first law degree with honours through the University of London's External Programme — a path where I was both the teacher and the student. I taught myself the law. There were no daily lectures, no built-in structure, no professor to reassure me that I belonged. There was only discipline, persistence, and the quiet resolve to keep going even when the material felt distant and unforgiving. Years later, I went on to earn my Master of Laws from an ABA-approved law school. By then, I had crossed jurisdictions, crossed borders, and crossed life stages. I was a mother. I had young children. I had studied law once, long ago, and returned to it again in a new country, under a new system, with new expectations.

I remember struggling in a class and asking a question — only to be told, *"Oh, you're a foreign student. That makes sense that you don't understand this.* "In that moment, the issue was no longer doctrine. It was belonging. That experience stayed with me.

- I know what it feels like to teach yourself law.
- I know what it feels like to move between legal systems.
- I know what it feels like to return to study after years away, carrying responsibility, doubt, and the quiet fear of wondering whether you still belong in the room.

Law in Pieces was born from that lived experience. This series is for those who are teaching themselves the law. For those who have studied in one jurisdiction and find themselves learning in another. For those who learn best through narrative, analogy, and connection rather than cold abstraction. For those who have ever felt isolated, incompetent, or tempted to second-guess their journey. These books are not shortcuts. They are bridges. They are designed to make doctrine human — to show how the law fits into real life, real harm, real relationships, and real choices. Each volume breaks complex rules into recognizable patterns, intuitive structures, and stories that stay with you long after the page is turned.

I do not believe the law is meant to be exclusionary. I do not believe confusion is a measure of intelligence. And I do not believe that struggling means you do not belong.
Law in Pieces exists to say: **you do belong**. Wherever you are studying from. However you arrived here. Whatever your path has looked like. These books are for you.

Warmly,
Anjanette G. Seymour, LL.M., LL.B. (Hons.)

Introduction

Introduction: The Power to Hear

Subject-matter jurisdiction is the bloodstream of the federal judiciary. Without it, nothing moves. No complaint breathes. No motion pulses. No judgment survives. If Personal Jurisdiction asks, *"Can this court reach this defendant?"* then Subject-Matter Jurisdiction asks the more existential question: **"Does this court have the power to hear this case at all?"**

This volume places that question under the scalpel.

Federal courts are courts of limited jurisdiction. They do not roam freely across disputes like generalist state courts. They operate within boundaries drawn by two hands:

- **The Constitution (Article III)** — the outer perimeter of federal judicial power.
- **Congress (statutes like §§ 1331, 1332, 1367, 1441)** — the precise vessels through which that power flows.

A federal court must have both. A constitutional heartbeat. A statutory artery. Only then does the case live.

And unlike Personal Jurisdiction, which parties may waive or forfeit, **Subject-Matter Jurisdiction is non-waivable**. It is the court's own oxygen supply. A defect suffocates the entire proceeding, no matter how late discovered. Even a final judgment could collapse if the court lacked jurisdiction from the start.

This book dissects that power.

We will examine the organs of federal jurisdiction — **Federal Question, Diversity, Supplemental Jurisdiction, and Removal** — not as abstract doctrines but as living systems. Each case is a patient. Each opinion is a surgical report. Each doctrinal rule is an anatomical structure that must be understood, traced, and respected.

You will see how a simple train-ticket dispute in *Mottley* reshaped the very definition of a federal question. How a married couple in *Mas v. Perry* clarified citizenship in ways that still echo today. How *Gibbs*, *Finley*, and § 1367 form the lungs through which supplemental claims breathe. How *Caterpillar v. Lewis* teaches that sometimes a jurisdictional defect can be cured — and sometimes it cannot.

By the end of this volume, you will not merely "know" Subject-Matter Jurisdiction. You will **see** it. You will **feel** its architecture. You will be able to diagnose its defects with the precision of a surgeon.

Welcome to the operating room.

The Purpose of This Book

Before you begin the case dissections, it helps to understand the purpose and design of this volume. This book is not meant to overwhelm you with doctrine — it is meant to guide you through it with clarity, structure, and confidence.

Subject-Matter Jurisdiction can feel intimidating because it is both technical and foundational. This book transforms that complexity into something you can see, understand, and use.

Here is how this volume is built to support you:

• It gives you a clear path.

Cases appear in chronological order so you can watch the doctrine evolve like a living body.

• It uses a consistent anatomical method.

Only the facts that matter survive the scalpel. Only the reasoning that shapes the doctrine is highlighted.

• It prepares you for real use.

• It shows you the whole body.

The Synthesis Chapter and flowcharts reveal how the pieces fit together into a coherent system.

• It empowers you.

This book is designed to make you feel capable, prepared, and grounded — not overwhelmed.

The purpose of this book is simple: to help you understand Subject-Matter Jurisdiction from the inside out, one careful dissection at a time.

Subject-Matter Jurisdiction: An Anatomical Introduction

The Anatomy of SMJ: Power, Pathways, and Limits

Subject-matter jurisdiction is not a single organ. It is a system — a network of vessels, chambers, and regulatory gates that determine whether a federal court may hear a case. To understand it, we must dissect it the way a surgeon studies the human body: organ by organ, function by function, pathology by pathology.

Below is the anatomical map that will guide every case dissection in this volume.

I. The Heart — The Source of Federal Judicial Power

Every system needs a heart. For federal courts, that heart is **Article III of the Constitution**. It sets the outer boundary of federal judicial power — the maximum range of cases federal courts *may* hear.

But Article III is only the heartbeat. Congress supplies the arteries.

Federal courts cannot act unless Congress grants jurisdiction through statutes like:

- **28 U.S.C. § 1331** — Federal Question
- **28 U.S.C. § 1332** — Diversity
- **28 U.S.C. § 1367** — Supplemental Jurisdiction
- **28 U.S.C. § 1441–1447** — Removal & Remand

A case must satisfy both the constitutional heartbeat and the statutory artery. If either fails, the case flatlines.

And because SMJ is about *power*, not fairness, it is **non-waivable**. A court must raise defects **Sua Sponte**. Parties cannot consent to it. No amount of litigation effort can resuscitate a case that never had jurisdiction to begin with.

II. The Spine — The Structural Rules That Hold SMJ Upright

The spine gives structure. In SMJ, that structure comes from the core categories of federal jurisdiction:

1. Federal Question Jurisdiction (§ 1331)

Cases "arising under" federal law. But what counts as "arising under"? *Mottley* will show you how deceptively simple — and devastatingly strict — this rule is.

2. Diversity Jurisdiction (§ 1332)

Cases between citizens of different states with an amount in controversy exceeding $75,000. This spine has many vertebrae:

- Complete diversity
- Citizenship rules for individuals, corporations, and LLCs
- Aggregation rules
- The time-of-filing rule

3. Supplemental Jurisdiction (§ 1367)

The connective tissue that allows related claims to travel together. It is the circulatory system that keeps complex litigation alive.

4. Removal & Remand (§§ 1441–1447)

The spinal reflexes — the mechanisms that move cases between state and federal court.

These structural rules keep the system upright and coherent.

III. The Brain — The Logic That Interprets Jurisdiction

The brain governs interpretation. In SMJ, the brain is made of doctrines that tell courts *how* to think about jurisdiction:

- **The Well-Pleaded Complaint Rule**
- **The Mottley Rule**

- **Narrow construction of federal jurisdiction**
- **Congressional control over jurisdictional grants**
- **Embedded federal issue doctrine (Grable)**
- **The distinction between jurisdiction and merits**

These doctrines are the neural pathways that shape every judicial decision.

IV. The Lungs — How SMJ Breathes Across Claims

Supplemental jurisdiction is the respiratory system of federal litigation. It allows claims to breathe together, travel together, and survive together.

Before § 1367, courts relied on **pendent** and **ancillary** jurisdiction. Then came:

- **Gibbs** — the oxygen of "common nucleus of operative fact"
- **Finley** — the sudden constriction
- **§ 1367** — Congress restoring breath
- **Exxon Mobil v. Allapattah** — the modern lung capacity

This system determines whether a federal court can inhale a whole dispute or must exhale parts of it back to state court.

V. The Fractures — Where Doctrine Breaks and Courts Repair

Every system has weak points. In SMJ, fractures appear where doctrine meets real-world complexity:

- **Fraudulent joinder**
- **Minimal vs. complete diversity**
- **Citizenship of LLCs and partnerships**
- **Domestic relations & probate exceptions**

- **Federal ingredient doctrine**
- **Embedded federal issues**
- **Aggregation puzzles**
- **Caterpillar-style cured defects**

These fractures are where courts innovate, improvise, and sometimes contradict themselves. This book will show you how to diagnose each one.

VI. How to Use This Anatomy in Case Dissections

Every case in this volume will be dissected using the same surgical template:

- **Vitals**
- **Patient History**
- **Symptoms**
- **Diagnosis**
- **Surgical Procedure**
- **Organs Affected**
- **Complications**
- **Aftercare**
- **Takeaway for Students**

This anatomical map tells you which "organs" each case touches. By the end, you will not only understand SMJ — you will be able to *see* it as a living system.

I. Constitutional Foundations

Strawbridge v. Curtiss (1806)

The Birth of Complete Diversity

The Heart — The Core Issue

Does the diversity statute require **complete diversity**, meaning every plaintiff must be diverse from every defendant?

The Spine — The Rule of Law

Yes. Under the Judiciary Act, **complete diversity is required**. If even one plaintiff shares citizenship with one defendant, diversity jurisdiction collapses.

The Brain — The Court's Reasoning

- The Court interprets the statute **narrowly**, emphasizing Congress's intent to limit federal jurisdiction.
- It distinguishes statutory limits from constitutional power.
- It concludes that Congress chose a **strict, formalistic** approach to diversity.

The Lungs — The Doctrinal Test

A federal court has diversity jurisdiction only if:

1. **Every plaintiff** is diverse from
2. **Every defendant**

No overlap. No exceptions. No partial diversity.

The Stomach — Facts Digested

- Multiple plaintiffs sued multiple defendants.
- Some plaintiffs and defendants shared state citizenship.

- The Court had to decide whether this overlap destroyed jurisdiction.

The Skin — The Holding

Complete diversity is required. Shared citizenship between any opposing parties kills jurisdiction.

The Fractures — Weaknesses & Tensions

- The rule is **statutory**, not constitutional.
- Congress *could* change it — but hasn't.
- Creates tension with Article III, which allows **minimal diversity**.

The Toxicology Report — External Influences

- Early suspicion of federal courts.
- Desire to limit federal power.
- Political sensitivity around federal-state balance in the early Republic.

The Cause of Death — What This Case Replaced

It effectively killed any assumption that diversity jurisdiction could be broad or flexible.

The Future Prognosis — Legacy

- Still governs today.
- Forms the backbone of §1332 analysis.
- Shapes later cases like **Grupo Dataflux** and **Allapattah**.

Variable Manipulation — What Changes the Outcome?

- Add or remove a party → jurisdiction may appear or disappear.

- Change a party's domicile → outcome flips.
- Reframe the lawsuit to avoid non-diverse parties → jurisdiction restored.

Mini-Lab — Apply the Rule

P1 (WI) sues D1 (IL) and D2 (WI). Does diversity exist?

No. P1 and D2 share citizenship → Strawbridge kills jurisdiction.

Osborn v. Bank of the United States (1824)

The Constitutional Maximum: The Federal-Ingredient Theory

The Heart — The Core Issue

Does a case "arise under" federal law for Article III purposes if it contains **any federal ingredient**, even if the main claim is state law?

The Spine — The Rule of Law

Yes. A case arises under federal law if **any federal issue** is embedded in the dispute.

This is the broadest possible interpretation of Article III.

The Brain — The Court's Reasoning

- Marshall emphasizes the supremacy of federal law.
- Federal courts must be able to protect federal institutions.
- Even a small federal issue is enough to satisfy Article III.
- Distinguishes constitutional power from statutory limits.

The Lungs — The Doctrinal Test

A case satisfies Article III if:

1. A federal issue is present
2. That issue forms part of the case's structure
3. Federal interests are implicated

This is the **constitutional ceiling** for federal-question jurisdiction.

The Stomach — Facts Digested

- Ohio attempted to tax the Bank of the United States.
- The Bank sued state officials in federal court.

- The question: Does the presence of a federal charter create federal jurisdiction?

The Skin — The Holding

Yes. Any federal ingredient is enough to satisfy Article III.

The Fractures — Weaknesses & Tensions

- Extremely broad — too broad for modern statutory jurisdiction.
- Creates a gap between Article III and §1331.
- Later cases narrow the statutory test, not the constitutional one.

The Toxicology Report — External Influences

- Marshall Court's strong nationalism.
- Desire to protect federal institutions from state interference.
- Early shaping of federal supremacy.

The Cause of Death — What This Case Replaced

It killed the idea that federal-question jurisdiction must be narrow at the constitutional level.

The Future Prognosis — Legacy

- Still good law for constitutional analysis.
- Forms the **outer boundary** of federal power.
- Modern cases (Mottley, Grable, Gunn) define the **inner boundary** under §1331.

Variable Manipulation — What Changes the Outcome?

- Remove the federal charter → no federal ingredient.

- Make the dispute purely state law → Article III not satisfied.
- Add a federal defense → still not enough for §1331, but enough for Article III.

Mini-Lab — Apply the Rule

A federally chartered corporation sues a state official over a state tax. Does Article III allow jurisdiction?

Yes. The federal charter is a federal ingredient → Osborn satisfied.

II. Federal Question Jurisdiction

Louisville & Nashville Railroad Co. v. Mottley (1908):

Full Legal Autopsy

This is the cadaver that teaches federal question doctrine how to breathe.

Mottley is the case that gives Subject-Matter Jurisdiction its **brainstem**. It is the moment the doctrine learns to distinguish between:

- a federal issue that **creates** jurisdiction, and
- a federal issue that merely **appears** in the background.

This autopsy shows exactly why *Mottley* is the intellectual ancestor of every modern §1331 case.

Identification of the Body

- **Case:** *Louisville & Nashville Railroad Co. v. Mottley*
- **Citation:** 211 U.S. 149 (1908)
- **Doctrine:** Subject-Matter Jurisdiction
- **Organ System:** Federal Question (§ 1331)
- **Era:** Foundational — the birth of the Well-Pleaded Complaint Rule
- **Reason for Autopsy:** This cadaver establishes the rule that federal jurisdiction must appear **on the face of the plaintiff's complaint**, not in anticipated defenses. It is the doctrine's first breath.

External Examination

The body presents with:

- A Kentucky couple injured in a train accident
- A settlement granting them lifetime free passes

- A later federal statute banning free passes
- A railroad refusing to honor the agreement
- Plaintiffs suing in federal court
- Plaintiffs arguing that the railroad's **defense** would require interpreting federal law

The central question: **Does a federal issue in the defendant's anticipated defense create federal question jurisdiction?**

This is where the doctrine confronts the limits of federal judicial power.

Internal Examination

Heart (Core Issue)

Does a case "arise under" federal law when the **only federal issue appears in the defendant's anticipated defense**?

The Court slices directly into the organ of §1331.

Spine (Rule of Law)

The Well-Pleaded Complaint Rule: A federal question must appear on the **face of the plaintiff's properly pleaded complaint**.

Anticipated defenses do **not** create jurisdiction.

This spine supports every federal question case that follows.

Brain (Reasoning)

This is where the doctrine develops cognition — the ability to distinguish between:

1. Federal issues that create jurisdiction

→ Those appearing in the plaintiff's claim.

2. Federal issues that do *not* create jurisdiction

→ Those appearing only in defenses or replies.

The Court reasons:

- Plaintiffs cannot manufacture jurisdiction by predicting a federal defense.
- The complaint itself must rely on federal law.
- The plaintiff controls the complaint — and therefore controls jurisdiction.
- Federal courts must guard their limited power.
- Allowing defenses to create jurisdiction would swallow §1331 whole.

This is the moment SMJ becomes **defendant-neutral, statute-bound, and disciplined**.

Lungs (Tests Applied)

The doctrine breathes through:

- The Well-Pleaded Complaint Rule
- The "arising under" test
- The distinction between claims and defenses
- The principle of limited federal jurisdiction
- The need for predictable boundaries

These tests oxygenate the entire federal question system.

Stomach (Facts Digested)

The Court digests:

- The Mottleys' claim was purely contractual — a state-law claim.

- The federal statute banning free passes appeared only in the railroad's **defense**.
- Plaintiffs tried to preemptively raise the federal issue.
- The complaint did not rely on federal law.
- Therefore, §1331 was not satisfied.

These facts do not nourish federal jurisdiction.

Cause of Death (for Broad Federal Question Theory)

This case kills the idea that:

- A federal defense creates federal question jurisdiction
- Anticipated federal issues are enough
- Plaintiffs can plead around state law to enter federal court
- Federal courts may hear any case involving federal law somewhere in the background

Mottley ends the era of jurisdiction by implication.

Toxicology Report

External forces influencing the decision:

- Fear of federal courts becoming courts of general jurisdiction
- Desire to preserve state-court primacy
- Judicial caution about expanding §1331
- Structural federalism concerns
- The need for predictable, administrable boundaries

These toxins shape the doctrine's metabolism.

Fractures and Weak Points

Even this brain has fractures:

- What counts as a "federal ingredient"?
- How to treat embedded federal issues?
- What about state claims requiring federal interpretation?
- How to reconcile *Mottley* with *Grable* and *Gunn*?
- Does the rule encourage strategic pleading?

These fractures will later split open in *Grable.*

Surviving Relatives

Mottley strengthens:

- Article III limits
- The Well-Pleaded Complaint Rule
- The distinction between claims and defenses
- Narrow construction of federal jurisdiction
- The idea that plaintiffs control the complaint
- The structural integrity of §1331

It becomes the ancestor of all modern federal question doctrine.

Future Prognosis

This case remains essential because it:

- Defines the boundaries of federal question jurisdiction
- Prevents jurisdictional manipulation
- Anchors the modern "arising under" analysis
- Shapes *Grable*, *Merrell Dow*, and *Gunn*
- Protects federal courts from overreach

It is the doctrine's **first breath and permanent heartbeat**.

Variable Manipulation

Changing one fact changes the outcome:

- If the Mottleys' claim itself required interpreting federal law → jurisdiction.
- If Congress created a federal cause of action → jurisdiction.
- If the complaint pleaded a federal right → jurisdiction.
- If the railroad's conduct violated a federal statute directly → jurisdiction.

This teaches students how to diagnose §1331 precisely.

Mini Lab:

Suppose the Mottleys had sued *under* the federal statute banning free passes, claiming it violated their constitutional rights. Would §1331 jurisdiction exist?

American Well Works Co. v. Layne & Bowler Co. (1916)

Full Legal Autopsy — Subject-Matter Jurisdiction (Federal Question: The Creation Test)

This is the cadaver that teaches the doctrine the simplest, cleanest rule in all of SMJ: A suit "arises under" the law that **creates the cause of action**.

If *Osborn* is the cosmic expansion and *Merrell Dow* is the contraction, *American Well Works* is the **center of gravity** — the case that gives us the **Creation Test**, the default rule for §1331.

This is the doctrine's **heartbeat.**

Identification of the Body

- **Case:** *American Well Works Co. v. Layne & Bowler Co.*
- **Citation:** 241 U.S. 257 (1916)
- **Doctrine:** Subject-Matter Jurisdiction
- **Organ System:** Federal Question (§ 1331)
- **Era:** Holmes Court
- **Reason for Autopsy:** This cadaver establishes the **Creation Test**, the primary rule for determining whether a case "arises under" federal law.

External Examination

The body presents with:

- A state-law **defamation** claim
- The defendant allegedly telling customers that plaintiff's pumps infringed federal patents
- Plaintiff suing in state court
- Defendant removing to federal court
- A question about whether the federal patent issue embedded

in the defamation claim creates federal-question jurisdiction

The central question: **Does a state-law claim arise under federal law simply because it involves a federal patent issue?**

This is where the doctrine confronts the **default rule** of federal-question jurisdiction.

Internal Examination

Heart (Core Issue)

What does it mean for a case to "arise under" federal law?

Spine (Rule of Law: The Creation Test)

Justice Holmes gives us the iconic rule:

"A suit arises under the law that **creates the cause of action**."

This is the **Creation Test**, the primary rule for §1331.

If the cause of action is created by:

- **Federal law → federal question jurisdiction exists**
- **State law → no federal question jurisdiction**, even if federal issues appear inside the case

This spine supports the entire modern structure of §1331.

Brain (Reasoning)

This is where the doctrine develops its minimalist intelligence.

Holmes reasons:

- The plaintiff's claim is **defamation**, a state-law tort.
- The fact that the alleged defamation involves patent infringement does not change the nature of the claim.
- The federal patent issue is a **defense**, not the source of the cause of action.

- Therefore, the case does **not** arise under federal law.
- Federal courts cannot take jurisdiction simply because federal law is implicated.

The brain becomes clear: **The origin of the cause of action controls — not the ingredients inside it.**

Lungs (Tests Applied)

The doctrine breathes through:

- The Creation Test
- The distinction between claims and defenses
- The principle that federal issues inside state claims do not create §1331 jurisdiction
- The need for a simple, predictable rule
- The limits of federal-ingredient jurisdiction

These tests oxygenate the federal-question system.

Stomach (Facts Digested)

The Court digests:

- The claim was defamation
- Defamation is created by state law
- Patent law appeared only as a factual issue
- The federal issue was not the source of the right to sue
- Therefore, no federal jurisdiction existed

These facts starve federal jurisdiction.

Cause of Death (for the "Federal Issue = Federal Jurisdiction" Theory)

This case kills the idea that:

- Any federal issue creates federal-question jurisdiction
- Federal defenses can create §1331 jurisdiction
- State-law claims with federal ingredients belong in federal court
- Federal courts can hear cases simply because they involve patents

The doctrine becomes simple, bright-line, and claim-focused.

Toxicology Report

External forces influencing the decision:

- Holmes's preference for simple, predictable rules
- The need to prevent federal courts from absorbing state tort law
- Early 20th-century federalism
- The desire to limit federal caseloads
- The importance of distinguishing claims from defenses

These toxins shape the doctrine's metabolism.

Fractures and Weak Points

Even this elegant brain has fractures:

- What about state claims that *depend* on federal law?
- What about hybrid claims?
- What about federal issues that are substantial to the federal system?
- How to reconcile this with *Osborn*'s broad constitutional view?
- How to treat cases like *Grable* where the federal issue is

central?

These fractures will later split open in *Grable* and *Gunn.*

Surviving Relatives

American Well Works strengthens:

- The Creation Test
- The distinction between claims and defenses
- The narrowness of §1331
- The foundation for modern federal-question doctrine
- The baseline rule that *Grable* and *Gunn* refine

It becomes the doctrinal ancestor of all federal-question cases.

Future Prognosis

This case remains essential because it:

- Defines the default rule for §1331
- Anchors the modern federal-question framework
- Explains why most cases belong in state court
- Shapes the structure of embedded-issue doctrine
- Provides the starting point for *Grable* and *Gunn*

It is the doctrine's **heartbeat**.

Variable Manipulation

Changing one fact changes the outcome:

- If the plaintiff sued for patent infringement → federal jurisdiction
- If Congress created a federal defamation cause of action → federal jurisdiction

- If the federal issue were the source of the right → federal jurisdiction
- If the federal issue were merely evidence → no jurisdiction

This teaches students how to diagnose federal-question cases precisely.

Mini Lab

Suppose a plaintiff sues for state-law fraud, alleging the defendant lied about compliance with federal environmental regulations. Does the case arise under federal law under *American Well Works*?

Bell v. Hood (1946)

Full Legal Autopsy — Subject-Matter Jurisdiction (Federal Question Pleading Doctrine)

This is the cadaver that teaches the doctrine that jurisdiction and merits are separate organs — and you cannot collapse them.

If *American Well Works* gives us the **Creation Test**, *Bell v. Hood* gives us the **Non-Frivolous Federal Claim Rule** — the rule that prevents federal judges from dismissing cases at the jurisdictional stage simply because they think the plaintiff will lose.

This is the doctrine's **triage principle**.

Identification of the Body

- **Case:** *Bell v. Hood*
- **Citation:** 327 U.S. 678 (1946)
- **Doctrine:** Subject-Matter Jurisdiction
- **Organ System:** Federal Question (§ 1331)
- **Era:** Post-Holmes clarification
- **Reason for Autopsy:** This cadaver establishes that **a federal court has jurisdiction if the plaintiff pleads a federal**

cause of action — unless the claim is wholly insubstantial or frivolous.

External Examination

The body presents with:

- Plaintiffs suing FBI agents for violating their Fourth and Fifth Amendment rights
- Plaintiffs seeking **damages** for constitutional violations
- No explicit federal statute authorizing damages at the time
- The district court dismissing for lack of jurisdiction
- A question about whether the absence of a federal remedy destroys jurisdiction
- A need to separate **jurisdiction** from **merits**

The central question: **Does a federal court have jurisdiction when the plaintiff asserts a federal claim that might ultimately fail?**

This is where the doctrine confronts the **difference between having a claim and winning a claim**.

Internal Examination

Heart (Core Issue)

Does a federal court have §1331 jurisdiction when the plaintiff asserts a federal cause of action that may not actually exist?

Spine (Rule of Law)

The Court establishes the **Bell v. Hood Rule**:

A federal court has jurisdiction when the plaintiff pleads a claim "arising under" federal law **unless** the claim is:

- **wholly insubstantial,**
- **frivolous**, or

- **made solely for the purpose of obtaining jurisdiction**.

This spine prevents judges from dismissing cases prematurely.

Brain (Reasoning)

This is where the doctrine develops its procedural intelligence.

The Court reasons:

- Jurisdiction is determined by the **face of the complaint**.
- If the plaintiff asserts a federal right, jurisdiction exists.
- Whether the plaintiff actually has a remedy is a **merits question**, not a jurisdictional one.
- Courts must not collapse jurisdiction and merits.
- Only claims that are **obviously frivolous** fail at the jurisdictional stage.

The brain becomes clear: **If the federal claim is colorable, the court has jurisdiction — even if the claim will lose.**

Lungs (Tests Applied)

The doctrine breathes through:

- The non-frivolous federal claim rule
- The separation of jurisdiction and merits
- The face-of-the-complaint rule
- The need to prevent premature dismissals
- The importance of judicial economy

These tests oxygenate federal-question pleading.

Stomach (Facts Digested)

The Court digests:

- Plaintiffs alleged constitutional violations
- They sought damages (not yet recognized under Bivens)
- The claim might fail on the merits
- But it was not frivolous
- Therefore, jurisdiction existed

These facts nourish federal jurisdiction.

Cause of Death (for the "No Remedy = No Jurisdiction" Theory)

This case kills the idea that:

- A federal claim must be valid to create jurisdiction
- Courts can dismiss for lack of jurisdiction simply because the claim is weak
- The absence of a federal remedy destroys §1331 jurisdiction
- Jurisdiction and merits are the same inquiry

The doctrine becomes protective, procedural, and plaintiff-friendly.

Toxicology Report

External forces influencing the decision:

- The need to prevent judges from gatekeeping too aggressively
- The rise of constitutional tort claims
- The importance of access to federal courts
- The desire to maintain a clean separation between jurisdiction and merits
- The need for predictable pleading rules

These toxins shape the doctrine's metabolism.

Fractures and Weak Points

Even this protective brain has fractures:

- What counts as "wholly insubstantial"?
- How to treat borderline federal claims?
- What about implied causes of action?
- How to reconcile this with *Merrell Dow*?
- How to treat claims that are federal in name only?

These fractures will later split open in *Bivens* and *Gunn*.

Surviving Relatives

Bell v. Hood strengthens:

- The non-frivolous federal claim rule
- The separation of jurisdiction and merits
- The face-of-the-complaint doctrine
- The modern structure of §1331
- The foundation for *Mottley*, *Grable*, and *Gunn*

It becomes the doctrinal guardian of federal-question pleading.

Future Prognosis

This case remains essential because it:

- Prevents premature jurisdictional dismissals
- Protects access to federal courts
- Clarifies the meaning of "arising under"
- Anchors the modern pleading framework
- Ensures that weak claims still get their day in court

It is the doctrine's **triage principle**.

Variable Manipulation

Changing one fact changes the outcome:

- If the federal claim were frivolous → no jurisdiction
- If the claim were invented solely to get into federal court → no jurisdiction
- If the plaintiff pleaded only state-law claims → no jurisdiction
- If the federal claim were substantial → jurisdiction exists even if the claim fails

This teaches students how to diagnose federal-question pleading precisely.

Mini Lab

Suppose a plaintiff sues under a federal statute that clearly does not provide a private right of action. Is the claim dismissed for lack of jurisdiction or failure on the merits under *Bell v. Hood*?

Merrell Dow Pharmaceuticals Inc. v. Thompson (1986)

Full Legal Autopsy — Subject-Matter Jurisdiction (Embedded Federal Issue: Pre-Grable Contraction)

This is the cadaver that teaches the doctrine that a federal issue inside a state claim is not enough — unless Congress intended a federal cause of action.

If *Osborn* is the cosmic expansion and *Grable* is the calibrated microscope, *Merrell Dow* is the **contraction** — the case that pulls federal-question doctrine inward, insisting that **no federal cause of action = no §1331 jurisdiction**, even when federal law is central to the claim.

This is the doctrine's **restrictive lung**, the one that temporarily collapses the federal-ingredient theory.

Identification of the Body

- **Case:** *Merrell Dow Pharmaceuticals Inc. v. Thompson*
- **Citation:** 478 U.S. 804 (1986)
- **Doctrine:** Subject-Matter Jurisdiction
- **Organ System:** Federal Question (§ 1331) — Embedded Federal Issue
- **Era:** Pre-Grable contraction
- **Reason for Autopsy:** This cadaver establishes that **a federal issue embedded in a state-law claim does NOT create federal jurisdiction** when Congress did not provide a federal cause of action.

External Examination

The body presents with:

- A state-law tort claim alleging that a drug (Bendectin) caused birth defects
- Plaintiffs arguing that Merrell Dow violated the **Federal**

Food, Drug, and Cosmetic Act (FDCA)

- FDCA violations used as **evidence of negligence per se**
- No federal cause of action under the FDCA
- A question about whether the embedded federal violation creates §1331 jurisdiction
- A need to determine whether federal issues inside state torts belong in federal court

The central question: **Does a state-law claim "arise under" federal law when the federal statute provides no private right of action?**

This is where the doctrine confronts the limits of federal-ingredient jurisdiction.

Internal Examination

Heart (Core Issue)

Can a federal issue embedded in a state-law negligence claim create federal-question jurisdiction when Congress did not authorize a federal cause of action?

Spine (Rule of Law)

The Court establishes a restrictive rule:

When Congress does **not** provide a federal cause of action, the presence of a federal issue inside a state-law claim is **strong evidence** that Congress did **not** intend federal-question jurisdiction.

This is the **anti-federal-ingredient rule**.

Brain (Reasoning)

This is where the doctrine develops its cautious intelligence.

The Court reasons:

- Congress intentionally **did not** create a private right of action under the FDCA.

- Allowing federal jurisdiction anyway would undermine congressional intent.
- Federal courts would be flooded with state tort claims involving federal standards.
- The federal issue was not substantial enough to justify federal jurisdiction.
- State courts are competent to apply federal standards in negligence cases.

The brain becomes clear: **No federal cause of action → strong presumption against §1331 jurisdiction.**

Lungs (Tests Applied)

The doctrine breathes through:

- Congressional intent
- The absence of a federal cause of action
- The need to avoid federalizing state tort law
- The limits of federal-ingredient jurisdiction
- The importance of preserving state-court authority

These tests constrict the embedded-issue doctrine.

Stomach (Facts Digested)

The Court digests:

- FDCA violations were used as negligence per se
- FDCA provides no private right of action
- The federal issue was important to the parties but not to the federal system

- Allowing jurisdiction would open the floodgates
- Congress's silence was treated as intentional

These facts starve federal jurisdiction.

Cause of Death (for the Broad Federal-Ingredient Theory)

This case kills the idea that:

- Any federal issue inside a state claim creates §1331 jurisdiction
- Federal standards automatically confer federal jurisdiction
- Congress's silence is irrelevant
- State tort claims with federal elements belong in federal court

The doctrine becomes narrow, cautious, and deferential to Congress.

Toxicology Report

External forces influencing the decision:

- Fear of federal courts being overwhelmed by tort claims
- Judicial restraint in the 1980s
- Congressional silence on FDCA private rights
- The need to preserve state-court primacy in tort law
- The desire to avoid federal overreach

These toxins shape the doctrine's metabolism.

Fractures and Weak Points

Even this restrictive brain has fractures:

- What if the federal issue is extremely important?
- What if Congress's silence is ambiguous?

- What about uniformity concerns?
- How to treat federal regulatory schemes?
- How to reconcile this with *Osborn*'s broad constitutional view?

These fractures will later split open in *Grable*.

Surviving Relatives

Merrell Dow strengthens:

- The importance of congressional intent
- The narrowness of §1331
- The distinction between federal issues and federal causes of action
- The limits of the embedded-issue doctrine
- The foundation for *Gunn*'s substantiality analysis

It becomes the doctrinal parent of *Grable* — by opposition.

Future Prognosis

This case remains essential because it:

- Defines the pre-Grable limits of federal-question jurisdiction
- Anchors the importance of congressional intent
- Prevents federalization of state tort law
- Shapes the modern embedded-issue framework
- Provides the restrictive baseline that *Grable* later refines

It is the doctrine's **pre-Grable contraction**.

Variable Manipulation

Changing one fact changes the outcome:

- If the FDCA had a private right of action → federal jurisdiction
- If Congress expressly authorized federal suits → jurisdiction
- If the federal issue were substantial to the federal system → possible jurisdiction
- If the claim were purely state-law without federal standards → no jurisdiction

This teaches students how to diagnose embedded federal issues precisely.

Mini Lab

Suppose Congress amends the FDCA to create a private right of action. Would a negligence-per-se claim based on FDCA violations now arise under federal law?

Grable & Sons Metal Products, Inc. v. Darue Engineering & Manufacturing (2005)

Full Legal Autopsy — Subject-Matter Jurisdiction (Embedded Federal Issue Doctrine)

This is the cadaver that teaches the doctrine how to detect federal DNA inside a state-law body.

If *Mottley* taught the doctrine that federal defenses do not create jurisdiction, *Grable* teaches the doctrine the **exception** — the rare moment when a state-law claim is so infused with federal meaning that it becomes federal in substance.

This is the case that gives § 1331 its **microscope**.

Identification of the Body

- **Case:** *Grable & Sons Metal Products, Inc. v. Darue Engineering & Manufacturing*

- **Citation:** 545 U.S. 308 (2005)
- **Doctrine:** Subject-Matter Jurisdiction
- **Organ System:** Federal Question (§ 1331) — Embedded Federal Issue
- **Era:** Modern clarification
- **Reason for Autopsy:** This cadaver establishes the **four-part test** for when a state-law claim "arises under" federal law because it contains a substantial, disputed federal issue.

External Examination

The body presents with:

- A quiet title action — a **state-law claim**
- A dispute over whether the IRS properly notified Grable before seizing property
- A buyer (Darue) who purchased the property from the IRS
- A plaintiff arguing that the IRS violated federal tax-notice requirements
- A defendant removing the case to federal court
- A question about whether a state-law claim with a federal ingredient belongs in federal court

The central question: **When does a state-law claim "arise under" federal law because it requires resolving a federal issue?**

This is where the doctrine confronts the boundary between state and federal judicial power.

Internal Examination

Heart (Core Issue)

Does a state-law quiet title action "arise under" federal law when the outcome turns on the interpretation of a federal tax statute?

Spine (Rule of Law)

The Court establishes the **Embedded Federal Issue Test**:

A state-law claim arises under federal law when:

1. The federal issue is **necessarily raised**
2. The federal issue is **actually disputed**
3. The federal issue is **substantial**
4. Federal jurisdiction will not **disturb the federal-state balance**

These four vertebrae form the backbone of the federal-ingredient doctrine.

Brain (Reasoning)

This is where the doctrine develops its diagnostic intelligence.

The Court reasons:

- The quiet title claim **necessarily** required interpreting the federal tax-notice statute.
- The meaning of the federal statute was **actually disputed**.
- The federal government had a strong interest in the **uniform interpretation** of tax-collection procedures.
- Allowing jurisdiction would not open the floodgates — such cases are rare.
- The federal issue was substantial to the federal system, not just the parties.

The brain becomes clear: **A state-law claim can be federal in substance if the federal issue is central, disputed, and important to the federal system.**

Lungs (Tests Applied)

The doctrine breathes through:

- Necessarily raised federal issue
- Actual dispute
- Substantiality
- Federal-state balance
- The distinction between federal ingredients and federal defenses
- The need for uniform federal interpretation

These tests oxygenate the embedded-issue doctrine.

Stomach (Facts Digested)

The Court digests:

- The IRS seized Grable's property
- The dispute turned on whether the IRS complied with federal notice requirements
- The quiet title claim could not be resolved without interpreting federal law
- The federal government had a strong interest in tax-collection uniformity
- The case was rare and would not overwhelm federal courts

These facts nourish federal jurisdiction.

Cause of Death (for the Strict State-Law-Only Theory)

This case kills the idea that:

- State-law claims can never arise under federal law
- Only federal causes of action create § 1331 jurisdiction
- Embedded federal issues are irrelevant

- Federal courts cannot hear state-law claims with federal meaning

The doctrine becomes nuanced, flexible, and substance-focused.

Toxicology Report

External forces influencing the decision:

- The need for uniform federal tax enforcement
- The rise of hybrid state-federal claims
- The desire to prevent federal-question doctrine from collapsing into *Mottley* rigidity
- The need to avoid opening the floodgates
- The importance of federal interests in administrative procedures

These toxins shape the doctrine's metabolism.

Fractures and Weak Points

Even this brain has fractures:

- What counts as "substantial"?
- How to measure federal-state balance?
- What about federal issues embedded in tort claims?
- How to treat cases involving federal regulations?
- How to reconcile *Grable* with *Merrell Dow* and *Gunn*?

These fractures will later split open in *Gunn v. Minton.*

Surviving Relatives

Grable strengthens:

- The embedded federal issue doctrine

- The distinction between federal ingredients and federal defenses
- The modern interpretation of § 1331
- The need for uniform federal interpretation
- The balance between state and federal judicial roles

It becomes the doctrinal parent of *Gunn v. Minton.*

Future Prognosis

This case remains essential because it:

- Defines when state-law claims belong in federal court
- Clarifies the meaning of "arising under"
- Shapes modern federal-question doctrine
- Anchors the federal-ingredient analysis
- Provides the microscope for § 1331 cases

It is the doctrine's **federal-DNA detector**.

Variable Manipulation

Changing one fact changes the outcome:

- If the federal issue were not necessary → no jurisdiction
- If the federal issue were not disputed → no jurisdiction
- If the federal issue were minor or fact-bound → no jurisdiction
- If allowing jurisdiction would open floodgates → no jurisdiction

This teaches students how to diagnose embedded federal issues precisely.

Mini Lab

Suppose a state-law negligence claim requires proving that a defendant violated a federal safety regulation. Does this satisfy the *Grable* test?

Gunn v. Minton (2013)

Full Legal Autopsy — Subject-Matter Jurisdiction (Federal Ingredient Doctrine Refined)

This is the cadaver that teaches the doctrine when federal DNA is too weak to justify federal jurisdiction.

If *Grable* opened the door for state-law claims with embedded federal issues, *Gunn* teaches the doctrine how to **close that door** when the federal issue is not substantial to the federal system.

This is the case that gives §1331 its **filter**.

Identification of the Body

- **Case:** *Gunn v. Minton*
- **Citation:** 568 U.S. 251 (2013)
- **Doctrine:** Subject-Matter Jurisdiction
- **Organ System:** Federal Question (§ 1331) — Embedded Federal Issue
- **Era:** Post-Grable refinement
- **Reason for Autopsy:** This cadaver clarifies that not every state-law claim involving federal law belongs in federal court. The federal issue must be **substantial to the federal system**, not just to the parties.

External Examination

The body presents with:

- A legal malpractice claim — a **state-law tort**
- The underlying case involved a patent infringement suit
- The plaintiff arguing that his lawyers mishandled a patent argument
- The defendant arguing that malpractice belongs in state court

- A question about whether the embedded patent issue creates federal jurisdiction
- A need to apply the *Grable* test

The central question: **Does a state-law malpractice claim "arise under" federal patent law because it requires analyzing a patent issue?**

This is where the doctrine confronts the limits of federal-ingredient jurisdiction.

Internal Examination

Heart (Core Issue)

Is a federal issue embedded in a state-law malpractice claim substantial enough to create federal question jurisdiction?

Spine (Rule of Law)

The Court applies and **tightens** the *Grable* test:

A state-law claim arises under federal law only if the federal issue is:

1. **Necessarily raised**
2. **Actually disputed**
3. **Substantial** — *to the federal system as a whole*
4. **Resolvable in federal court without disrupting the federal-state balance**

The key vertebra here is **substantiality**.

Brain (Reasoning)

This is where the doctrine develops its systemic intelligence.

The Court reasons:

- The malpractice claim necessarily required analyzing patent law.

- The patent issue was actually disputed.
- But the issue was **not substantial to the federal system** — only to the parties.
- The malpractice decision would not control future patent cases.
- State courts routinely apply federal law in malpractice contexts.
- Allowing jurisdiction would shift a massive category of state claims into federal court.

The brain becomes clear: **A federal issue must matter to the federal system, not just to the litigants.**

Lungs (Tests Applied)

The doctrine breathes through:

- The full *Grable* four-part test
- The distinction between party-importance and system-importance
- The need to preserve state control over malpractice law
- The federal-state balance
- The principle that federal courts are not courts of general error correction

These tests oxygenate the refined embedded-issue doctrine.

Stomach (Facts Digested)

The Court digests:

- The malpractice claim was purely state-law
- The patent issue was relevant but not systemically important
- The outcome would not bind federal patent courts

- State courts are competent to apply patent law
- Federal jurisdiction would disrupt the balance of judicial responsibilities

These facts starve federal jurisdiction.

Cause of Death (for the Broad Embedded-Issue Theory)

This case kills the idea that:

- Any federal issue inside a state claim creates §1331 jurisdiction
- Patent issues automatically confer federal jurisdiction
- Substantiality means "important to the parties"
- State courts cannot apply federal law
- *Grable* is a wide-open door

The doctrine becomes narrow, disciplined, and system-focused.

Toxicology Report

External forces influencing the decision:

- Fear of federal courts being flooded with malpractice cases
- The need to preserve state control over professional-responsibility law
- The importance of federal-state balance
- The rise of hybrid state-federal claims
- The desire to prevent jurisdictional overreach

These toxins shape the doctrine's metabolism.

Fractures and Weak Points

Even this refined brain has fractures:

- What counts as "substantial to the federal system"?
- How to treat federal regulatory issues in state torts?
- What about state claims involving federal constitutional questions?
- How to treat claims that indirectly affect federal agencies?
- How to reconcile *Gunn* with *Grable* in close cases?

These fractures continue to challenge lower courts.

Surviving Relatives

Gunn strengthens:

- The narrowness of the embedded-issue doctrine
- The distinction between federal importance and party importance
- The federal-state balance
- The modern interpretation of § 1331
- The limits of *Grable*

It becomes the doctrinal child of *Grable* and the guardian of §1331 boundaries.

Future Prognosis

This case remains essential because it:

- Defines the limits of federal-ingredient jurisdiction
- Prevents federal courts from absorbing state malpractice law
- Clarifies the meaning of "substantial"
- Anchors the modern *Grable* framework
- Protects the federal-state balance

It is the doctrine's **federal-issue filter**.

Variable Manipulation

Changing one fact changes the outcome:

- If the federal issue controlled future patent cases → jurisdiction
- If Congress created a federal malpractice cause of action → jurisdiction
- If the state claim required resolving a novel federal question → possible jurisdiction
- If the federal issue were minor or hypothetical → no jurisdiction

This teaches students how to diagnose embedded federal issues precisely.

Mini Lab

Suppose a state-law malpractice claim turns on whether the lawyer failed to raise a novel constitutional argument that no court has addressed. Does this satisfy the *Gunn* substantiality requirement?

III. Diversity Jurisdiction

St. Paul Mercury Indemnity Co. v. Red Cab Co. (1938)

Full Legal Autopsy — Subject-Matter Jurisdiction (Diversity: Amount in Controversy)

This is the cadaver that teaches the doctrine how to measure the heart pressure of a lawsuit.

If *Mas v. Perry* taught the doctrine who the parties are, *St. Paul Mercury* teaches the doctrine **how much the case is worth** — and when that value is enough to open the doors of federal court.

This is the case that gives the amount-in-controversy requirement its **pulse**.

Identification of the Body

- **Case:** *St. Paul Mercury Indemnity Co. v. Red Cab Co.*
- **Citation:** 303 U.S. 283 (1938)
- **Doctrine:** Subject-Matter Jurisdiction
- **Organ System:** Diversity Jurisdiction — Amount in Controversy (§ 1332)
- **Era:** Foundational clarification
- **Reason for Autopsy:** This cadaver establishes the **legal certainty test** and teaches the doctrine when a plaintiff's claimed damages control — and when they do not.

External Examination

The body presents with:

- A plaintiff who originally claimed damages exceeding the jurisdictional minimum
- A defendant who removed the case to federal court
- A plaintiff who then **reduced** the damages claim below the

threshold

- A question about whether post-removal changes destroy jurisdiction
- A need to determine whether the amount in controversy was met at filing

The central question: **Can a plaintiff defeat federal jurisdiction by lowering the damages after removal?**

This is where the doctrine confronts the timing and integrity of jurisdictional value.

Internal Examination

Heart (Core Issue)

Does the amount in controversy depend on the plaintiff's claim **at the time of filing**, or can later reductions eliminate federal jurisdiction?

Spine (Rule of Law)

The Court establishes the **Legal Certainty Test**:

The sum claimed by the plaintiff controls **if** the claim is made in good faith. Jurisdiction exists unless it appears **to a legal certainty** that the claim is really for less than the jurisdictional amount.

And:

Post-filing or post-removal reductions do not destroy jurisdiction.

These vertebrae support all modern amount-in-controversy analysis.

Brain (Reasoning)

This is where the doctrine develops its economic intelligence.

The Court reasons:

- Jurisdiction is determined **at the moment of filing**.

- Plaintiffs cannot manipulate jurisdiction by lowering damages after removal.
- The federal courts must rely on the plaintiff's good-faith valuation.
- Only if it is **legally impossible** for the plaintiff to recover the jurisdictional amount may the case be dismissed.
- Allowing post-removal reductions would encourage gamesmanship.

The brain becomes clear: **Jurisdictional value is fixed at filing and insulated from later strategic behavior.**

Lungs (Tests Applied)

The doctrine breathes through:

- The legal certainty test
- The time-of-filing rule
- Good-faith pleading
- Limits on post-removal manipulation
- The principle that jurisdiction, once attached, is not easily lost

These tests oxygenate the amount-in-controversy system.

Stomach (Facts Digested)

The Court digests:

- Plaintiff's original claim exceeded the jurisdictional minimum
- Defendant removed properly
- Plaintiff later amended the claim downward
- The amendment was irrelevant to jurisdiction
- The original claim was made in good faith

- There was no legal certainty the plaintiff could not recover the higher amount

These facts nourish federal jurisdiction.

Cause of Death (for Post-Removal Manipulation Theory)

This case kills the idea that:

- Plaintiffs can defeat removal by lowering damages
- Jurisdiction fluctuates with amended pleadings
- Courts must reevaluate amount in controversy after filing
- Strategic pleading can control federal power

The doctrine becomes stable, predictable, and resistant to manipulation.

Toxicology Report

External forces influencing the decision:

- Fear of plaintiffs gaming the system
- Desire for predictable jurisdictional rules
- Federalism concerns
- The need for administrative efficiency
- The importance of preventing forum shopping

These toxins shape the doctrine's metabolism.

Fractures and Weak Points

Even this brain has fractures:

- What counts as "good faith"?
- How to treat punitive damages?
- What about attorney's fees?

- How to value injunctions?
- What about class actions?
- How to treat ambiguous complaints?

These fractures will later split open in modern valuation cases.

Surviving Relatives

St. Paul Mercury strengthens:

- The time-of-filing rule
- The legal certainty test
- The stability of federal jurisdiction
- The integrity of removal
- The principle that plaintiffs cannot manipulate jurisdiction post-filing

It becomes the doctrinal parent of all modern amount-in-controversy cases.

Future Prognosis

This case remains essential because it:

- Defines how to measure the value of a case
- Prevents jurisdictional manipulation
- Anchors removal practice
- Shapes modern diversity analysis
- Provides a clear, administrable standard

It is the doctrine's **circulatory pressure regulator**.

Variable Manipulation

Changing one fact changes the outcome:

- If the original claim was below the threshold → no jurisdiction
- If the plaintiff pleaded the amount in bad faith → dismissal
- If state law capped damages below the threshold → legal certainty test fails
- If punitive damages were unavailable → amount may drop below minimum

This teaches students how to diagnose amount-in-controversy precisely.

Mini Lab

Suppose a plaintiff claims $100,000 in damages, but state law caps recovery at $50,000. Does federal jurisdiction exist under *St. Paul Mercury*?

Mas v. Perry (1974)

Full Legal Autopsy — Subject-Matter Jurisdiction (Diversity)

This is the cadaver that teaches the doctrine how to identify citizenship.

If *Mottley* gave SMJ its brainstem, *Mas v. Perry* gives it its **identity**. This is the case that teaches students how to determine **who a person is** for jurisdictional purposes — not emotionally, not culturally, but legally.

It is the doctrine's first lesson in **domicile, marriage**, and **the permanence of intent**.

Identification of the Body

- **Case:** *Mas v. Perry*
- **Citation:** 489 F.2d 1396 (5th Cir. 1974)
- **Doctrine:** Subject-Matter Jurisdiction

- **Organ System:** Diversity Jurisdiction (§ 1332)
- **Era:** Modern clarification of domicile
- **Reason for Autopsy:** This cadaver teaches the doctrine how to determine **citizenship**, how to treat **marriage**, and how to apply the **time-of-filing rule**. It is the backbone of diversity analysis.

External Examination

The body presents with:

- A married couple: Mrs. Mas (a French citizen) and Mr. Mas (a Mississippi citizen)
- A landlord in Louisiana who secretly installed two-way mirrors
- A lawsuit filed in federal court
- A question about whether diversity jurisdiction exists
- A dispute over Mrs. Mas's domicile after marriage
- A need to determine whether the couple is diverse from the Louisiana defendant

The central question: **Where is a married woman domiciled for purposes of §1332?**

This is where the doctrine confronts the meaning of identity.

Internal Examination

Heart (Core Issue)

What is the domicile — and therefore the citizenship — of a married woman who has not yet established a permanent home in the United States?

Spine (Rule of Law)

The Court reinforces three structural rules:

1. **Citizenship = Domicile** - Domicile requires:
    - Physical presence
    - Intent to remain indefinitely
2. **Marriage does not automatically change domicile** A woman does **not** take her husband's domicile by operation of law.
3. **Time-of-Filing Rule** Jurisdiction is determined **at the moment the complaint is filed**.

These vertebrae support all diversity analysis.

Brain (Reasoning)

This is where the doctrine develops its analytical intelligence.

The Court reasons:

- Mrs. Mas was a **French citizen** who had not established a U.S. domicile.
- She had lived in Louisiana only temporarily as a graduate student.
- She had no intent to remain there indefinitely.
- Marriage to a Mississippi citizen did not automatically make her a Mississippi domiciliary.
- Therefore, she remained a **citizen of France** for diversity purposes.
- Mr. Mas was a **citizen of Mississippi**.
- The defendant was a **citizen of Louisiana**.
- Complete diversity existed.

The brain becomes clear: **Domicile is about intent, not marriage, not residency, not convenience.**

Lungs (Tests Applied)

The doctrine breathes through:

- Physical presence + intent to remain
- Citizenship of individuals
- Citizenship of aliens
- Complete diversity requirement
- Time-of-filing rule
- No automatic transfer of domicile through marriage

These tests oxygenate the diversity system.

Stomach (Facts Digested)

The Court digests:

- Mrs. Mas's French citizenship
- Her temporary presence in Louisiana
- Her lack of intent to remain
- Mr. Mas's Mississippi domicile
- The defendant's Louisiana citizenship
- The timing of the lawsuit

These facts nourish diversity jurisdiction.

Cause of Death (for the Old Marital Domicile Rule)

This case kills the idea that:

- A woman automatically takes her husband's domicile
- Temporary residence equals domicile
- Students can rely on outdated common-law marital rules

- Intent is irrelevant to citizenship
- Diversity can be destroyed by marriage

The doctrine becomes modern, autonomous, and identity-based.

Toxicology Report

External forces influencing the decision:

- The decline of coverture
- Modern recognition of women's legal independence
- Federalism concerns
- The need for predictable citizenship rules
- The rise of international marriages and mobility
- The importance of clear diversity boundaries

These toxins shape the doctrine's metabolism.

Fractures and Weak Points

Even this brain has fractures:

- What counts as "intent to remain indefinitely"?
- How to treat students, military members, and temporary workers?
- What about couples who move frequently?
- How to treat dual citizens?
- How to treat undocumented individuals?

These fractures will later split open in modern domicile cases.

Surviving Relatives

Mas v. Perry strengthens:

- The modern definition of domicile
- The independence of spousal citizenship
- The time-of-filing rule
- The complete diversity requirement
- The treatment of aliens under §1332(a)(2)

It becomes the doctrinal parent of all modern domicile cases.

Future Prognosis

This case remains essential because it:

- Defines citizenship for diversity
- Clarifies the role of intent
- Modernizes domicile doctrine
- Protects federal courts from jurisdictional manipulation
- Shapes analysis in every diversity case that follows

It is the doctrine's **identity center**.

Variable Manipulation

Changing one fact changes the outcome:

- If Mrs. Mas intended to remain in Louisiana → Louisiana citizen
- If she had moved permanently to Mississippi → Mississippi citizen
- If the defendant were from Mississippi → no diversity
- If the couple filed after moving → time-of-filing rule changes nothing

This teaches students how to diagnose domicile precisely.

Mini Lab

Suppose Mrs. Mas had signed a long-term lease in Louisiana and told friends she planned to stay indefinitely. Would she still be a French citizen for diversity purposes?

Grupo Dataflux v. Atlas Global Group, L.P. (2004)

Full Legal Autopsy — Subject-Matter Jurisdiction (Time-of-Filing Rule for Diversity)

This is the cadaver that teaches the doctrine that jurisdiction is determined at the moment of filing — and nothing that happens afterward can resurrect a dead case.

If *Caterpillar* taught the doctrine that some defects can be cured, *Grupo Dataflux* teaches the doctrine the opposite: **A defect in diversity at the time of filing is fatal and cannot be cured by later changes in party citizenship.**

This is the case that gives diversity jurisdiction its **clock**.

Identification of the Body

- **Case:** *Grupo Dataflux v. Atlas Global Group, L.P.*
- **Citation:** 541 U.S. 567 (2004)
- **Doctrine:** Subject-Matter Jurisdiction
- **Organ System:** Diversity Jurisdiction — Time-of-Filing Rule
- **Era:** Modern reaffirmation
- **Reason for Autopsy:** This cadaver reaffirms the **time-of-filing rule** and rejects attempts to cure diversity defects by changing party citizenship after the lawsuit begins.

External Examination

The body presents with:

- A partnership (Atlas) suing a Mexican corporation (Grupo Dataflux)
- Some partners of Atlas were Mexican citizens at the time of filing
- This destroyed complete diversity

- During litigation, the non-diverse partners left the partnership
- Atlas argued that diversity was now complete
- A question about whether this post-filing change cured the defect
- A need to determine whether diversity can be fixed retroactively

The central question: **Can a diversity defect at the time of filing be cured by later changes in party citizenship?**

This is where the doctrine confronts the rigidity of jurisdictional timing.

Internal Examination

Heart (Core Issue)

Does the time-of-filing rule prohibit curing a diversity defect by changing the citizenship of parties after the lawsuit begins?

Spine (Rule of Law)

The Court reaffirms a strict rule:

Diversity jurisdiction is determined at the moment the complaint is filed. Later changes in party citizenship **cannot** cure a jurisdictional defect.

This spine is one of the oldest and strongest in federal jurisdiction.

Brain (Reasoning)

This is where the doctrine develops its temporal intelligence.

The Court reasons:

- Diversity must exist at the time of filing — not later.

- A partnership's citizenship depends on **all** its partners.
- Because some partners were Mexican citizens at filing, diversity was destroyed.
- Their later departure did not retroactively create jurisdiction.
- Jurisdiction cannot be created by post-filing events.
- Allowing such cures would undermine the stability of jurisdictional rules.

The brain becomes clear: **Jurisdiction is fixed in time — not fluid.**

Lungs (Tests Applied)

The doctrine breathes through:

- The time-of-filing rule
- The complete diversity requirement
- The citizenship rules for partnerships
- The distinction between curing procedural defects and curing jurisdictional defects
- The principle that subject-matter jurisdiction cannot be waived or created by consent

These tests oxygenate the timing doctrine.

Stomach (Facts Digested)

The Court digests:

- Atlas was a partnership with Mexican partners
- Grupo Dataflux was a Mexican corporation
- Diversity was incomplete at filing
- The later departure of the Mexican partners did not change the past

- The defect was jurisdictional, not procedural
- The case had to be dismissed

These facts starve jurisdiction.

Cause of Death (for the Post-Filing Cure Theory)

This case kills the idea that:

- Diversity defects can be cured by changing party citizenship
- Jurisdiction can be created retroactively
- Partnerships can manipulate membership to create jurisdiction
- Post-filing events matter for SMJ
- Time-of-filing is flexible

The doctrine becomes rigid, historical, and uncompromising.

Toxicology Report

External forces influencing the decision:

- The need for predictable jurisdictional rules
- Fear of manipulation by partnerships and LLCs
- The rise of complex business entities
- The importance of maintaining federal-state boundaries
- Judicial caution about expanding federal jurisdiction

These toxins shape the doctrine's metabolism.

Fractures and Weak Points

Even this rigid brain has fractures:

- What about dropping a non-diverse party entirely (Rule 21)?

- What about misjoinder?
- What about fraudulent joinder?
- What about class actions under CAFA?
- How to treat citizenship changes due to mergers or dissolutions?

These fractures continue to challenge lower courts.

Surviving Relatives

Grupo Dataflux strengthens:

- The time-of-filing rule
- The complete diversity requirement
- The distinction between jurisdictional and procedural defects
- The citizenship rules for partnerships
- The stability of federal jurisdiction

It becomes the doctrinal guardian of temporal integrity.

Future Prognosis

This case remains essential because it:

- Defines the temporal boundaries of diversity jurisdiction
- Prevents manipulation of party citizenship
- Anchors the time-of-filing rule
- Shapes modern partnership and LLC litigation
- Protects the federal-state balance

It is the doctrine's **clock**.

Variable Manipulation

Changing one fact changes the outcome:

- If the non-diverse partners had been dropped **before filing** → jurisdiction
- If the plaintiff were a corporation instead of a partnership → different citizenship rules
- If the non-diverse party were dismissed under Rule 21 → possible cure
- If diversity existed at filing but was later destroyed → jurisdiction remains

This teaches students how to diagnose timing precisely.

Mini Lab

Suppose a non-diverse partner is dismissed under Rule 21 for misjoinder after filing. Does this cure the diversity defect under *Grupo Dataflux*?

Hertz Corp. v. Friend (2010)

Full Legal Autopsy — Subject-Matter Jurisdiction (Diversity: Corporate Citizenship)

This is the cadaver that teaches the doctrine where a corporation "lives."

If *Mas v. Perry* taught the doctrine how to identify **people**, *Hertz* teaches it how to identify **corporations**. This is the case that gives diversity jurisdiction its **nerve center** — literally.

It is the doctrine's answer to the chaos of multi-state corporations and the need for a single, predictable test.

Identification of the Body

- **Case:** *Hertz Corp. v. Friend*
- **Citation:** 559 U.S. 77 (2010)
- **Doctrine:** Subject-Matter Jurisdiction
- **Organ System:** Diversity Jurisdiction (§ 1332(c)(1))
- **Era:** Modern clarification of corporate citizenship
- **Reason for Autopsy:** This cadaver establishes the **nerve center test**, giving courts a clear, uniform way to determine a corporation's principal place of business.

External Examination

The body presents with:

- A class action filed in California state court
- Plaintiffs claiming Hertz was a California citizen
- Hertz seeking removal to federal court
- Confusion over where Hertz's "principal place of business" was
- Competing tests across circuits (place of operations vs. nerve

center)

- A need for a single, national rule

The central question: **Where is a corporation "from" for purposes of diversity jurisdiction?**

This is where the doctrine confronts the identity of modern corporations.

Internal Examination

Heart (Core Issue)

What is the correct test for determining a corporation's **principal place of business** under §1332(c)(1)?

Spine (Rule of Law)

The Court establishes the **Nerve Center Test**:

A corporation's principal place of business is the place where its **high-level officers direct, control, and coordinate the corporation's activities** — typically its headquarters.

This spine replaces decades of fractured, inconsistent tests.

Brain (Reasoning)

This is where the doctrine develops its executive function — the ability to locate the "mind" of a corporation.

The Court reasons:

- Congress intended a **single, simple, predictable** test.
- The "place of operations" test created inconsistent results.
- Corporations need a rule they can apply without litigation.
- The nerve center reflects the corporation's **actual direction and control**.
- The headquarters is usually the best proxy — unless it is a

sham.

- The test must be **administrable**, not metaphysical.

The brain becomes clear: **A corporation has one home brain, not many operational limbs.**

Lungs (Tests Applied)

The doctrine breathes through:

- The nerve center test
- The headquarters presumption
- The requirement of actual direction and control
- The rejection of multi-factor balancing
- The need for predictability in jurisdiction
- The avoidance of forum manipulation

These tests oxygenate corporate citizenship doctrine.

Stomach (Facts Digested)

The Court digests:

- Hertz's headquarters was in New Jersey
- High-level officers worked and directed operations from New Jersey
- California had many operations, but not the corporate "brain"
- Plaintiffs relied on the "place of operations" test
- The Court rejected that approach in favor of uniformity

These facts nourish the nerve center conclusion.

Cause of Death (for the Old Multi-Factor Tests)

This case kills the idea that:

- A corporation's principal place of business is where it does the most business
- Operational volume determines citizenship
- Courts should use complex, circuit-specific balancing tests
- Corporations can have multiple principal places of business
- Citizenship should be determined by economic footprint

The doctrine becomes simple, centralized, and predictable.

Toxicology Report

External forces influencing the decision:

- National corporations operating in all 50 states
- Forum shopping concerns
- The need for uniform federal rules
- Administrative efficiency
- The rise of class actions and mass torts
- Congressional intent to limit federal jurisdiction

These toxins shape the doctrine's metabolism.

Fractures and Weak Points

Even this brain has fractures:

- What if the headquarters is nominal or symbolic?
- What if executives work remotely?
- What about corporations with decentralized leadership?
- How to treat holding companies?

- What about companies with dual headquarters?

These fractures will later split open in modern remote-work and multinational cases.

Surviving Relatives

Hertz strengthens:

- The complete diversity requirement
- The modern definition of corporate citizenship
- The time-of-filing rule
- Predictability in removal
- The distinction between operations and control
- The uniformity Congress intended in §1332(c)(1)

It becomes the doctrinal parent of all modern corporate citizenship cases.

Future Prognosis

This case remains essential because it:

- Defines corporate citizenship
- Simplifies diversity analysis
- Reduces forum shopping
- Provides a uniform national rule
- Anchors modern removal practice
- Shapes analysis in every corporate diversity case

It is the doctrine's **executive brain**.

Variable Manipulation

Changing one fact changes the outcome:

- If Hertz's executives actually directed operations from California → California citizen
- If the headquarters were a sham → nerve center elsewhere
- If the corporation had dual headquarters → fact-intensive inquiry
- If the company decentralized leadership → nerve center harder to locate

This teaches students how to diagnose corporate citizenship precisely.

Mini Lab

Suppose a corporation's headquarters is in Illinois, but all major decisions are made by executives working remotely from Texas. Under *Hertz*, where is the corporation's principal place of business?

IV. Supplemental Jurisdiction

United Mine Workers v. Gibbs (1966)

Full Legal Autopsy — Subject-Matter Jurisdiction (Supplemental Jurisdiction)

This is the cadaver that teaches the doctrine how to breathe.

If *Mottley* gave SMJ its **brainstem** and *Mas* gave **it identity,** *Gibbs* gives **it lungs — the ability to inhale related state-law claims and exhale those that do not belong.**

This is the case that creates the **"common nucleus of operative fact" test — the oxygen of modern supplemental jurisdiction.**

Identification of the Body

- **Case:** *United Mine Workers v. Gibbs*
- **Citation:** 383 U.S. 715 (1966)
- **Doctrine:** Subject-Matter Jurisdiction
- **Organ System:** Supplemental Jurisdiction (pre-§1367)
- **Era: Foundational** — the birth of modern pendent jurisdiction
- **Reason for Autopsy:** This cadaver establishes the test for when federal courts may hear state-law claims alongside federal ones.

External Examination

The body presents with:

- A labor dispute in Tennessee
- A plaintiff with both federal and state claims
- Federal claims under §303 of the LMRA
- State-law claims for interference with contract

- A jury verdict awarding damages on both
- A question about whether the federal court had power to hear the state claims
- A need for a unifying test

The central question: **When may a federal court hear state-law claims that accompany a federal claim?**

This is where the doctrine confronts the boundaries of federal judicial efficiency.

Internal Examination

Heart (Core Issue)

Do federal courts have jurisdiction over state-law claims **that arise from the same events as a federal claim?**

Spine (Rule of Law)

The Court establishes **the Common Nucleus of Operative Fact Test:**

Federal courts may hear state-law claims **when they arise from a common nucleus of operative fact with the federal claim** and are such that **a plaintiff would ordinarily try them in one proceeding.**

And:

Supplemental jurisdiction is discretionary, not mandatory.

These vertebrae support all modern supplemental jurisdiction analysis.

Brain (Reasoning)

This is where the doctrine develops its respiratory intelligence.

The Court reasons:

- Judicial economy favors hearing **related claims together.**
- Federal courts should **avoid piecemeal litigation**.
- But federal courts must **not overreach into state-law territory.**
- The key is factual relatedness — **not legal similarity.**
- The federal claim **must be substantial.**
- Even when jurisdiction exists, **courts may decline it for prudential reasons.**

The brain becomes clear: Supplemental jurisdiction is about factual unity, not legal overlap.

Lungs (Tests Applied)

The doctrine breathes through:

- Common nucleus of operative fact
- Substantiality of the federal claim
- Judicial economy
- Convenience
- Fairness
- Comity
- Discretion to decline jurisdiction

These tests oxygenate the supplemental jurisdiction system.

Stomach (Facts Digested)

The Court digests:

- The federal and state claims arose from the same labor dispute
- The same witnesses, evidence, and events were involved

- The federal claim was substantial
- The state claims were not separate or remote
- The trial court acted within its discretion

These facts nourish supplemental jurisdiction.

Cause of Death (for the Old Fragmented Litigation Theory)

This case kills the idea that:

- Federal courts must sever state-law claims
- Only legally related claims can be heard together
- Federal courts lack flexibility
- Supplemental jurisdiction is automatic or rigid

The doctrine becomes unified, efficient, and fact-centered.

Toxicology Report

External forces influencing the decision:

- The rise of complex litigation
- The need for efficient judicial administration
- Federalism concerns
- The desire to avoid duplicative trials
- The practical realities of labor disputes

These toxins shape the doctrine's metabolism.

Fractures and Weak Points

Even this brain has fractures:

- What counts as a "common nucleus"?
- How substantial must the federal claim be?

- When should courts decline jurisdiction?
- How to treat pendent parties?
- How to treat claims that arise later?

These fractures will later split open in *Finley* and lead to §1367.

Surviving Relatives

Gibbs strengthens:

- The modern concept of supplemental jurisdiction
- Judicial economy principles
- The discretionary nature of pendent claims
- The factual-relatedness standard
- The foundation for §1367(a)

It becomes the doctrinal parent of all supplemental jurisdiction cases.

Future Prognosis

This case remains essential because it:

- Defines the core test for supplemental jurisdiction
- Balances efficiency with federalism
- Anchors §1367's statutory framework
- Shapes modern multi-claim litigation
- Provides the lungs through which federal cases breathe

It is the doctrine's first breath of supplemental life.

Variable Manipulation

Changing one fact changes the outcome:

- If the federal claim were insubstantial → no supplemental

jurisdiction

- If the state claims arose from different events → no common nucleus
- If the federal claim were dismissed early → court may decline jurisdiction
- If the state claims dominated the case → discretion to decline

This teaches students how to diagnose supplemental jurisdiction precisely.

Mini Lab

Suppose the federal claim is dismissed at summary judgment, but the state claims remain. Under *Gibbs*, should the federal court keep the state claims?

Finley v. United States (1989)

Full Legal Autopsy — Subject-Matter Jurisdiction (Supplemental Jurisdiction Collapse)

This is the cadaver that teaches the doctrine what it cannot do.

If *Gibbs* gave supplemental jurisdiction its lungs, *Finley* is the moment those lungs collapse. This case is the suffocation that leads directly to Congress creating § 1367 — the statutory oxygen tank of modern supplemental jurisdiction.

Identification of the Body

- Case: *Finley v. United States*
- Citation: 490 U.S. 545 (1989)
- Doctrine: Subject-Matter Jurisdiction
- Organ System: Supplemental Jurisdiction (Pendent-Party Jurisdiction)
- Era: Pre-§1367 contraction
- Reason for Autopsy: This cadaver kills pendent-party jurisdiction unless Congress expressly authorizes it. It is the doctrinal crisis that triggers the birth of § 1367.

External Examination

The body presents with:

- A plane crash near a San Diego airport
- A widow suing the United States under the Federal Tort Claims Act (FTCA)
- Additional defendants: the city and the utility company
- A federal claim (FTCA) plus state-law claims against non-federal parties
- A question about whether the federal court can hear the

state-law claims against the additional defendants

- A need to determine whether *Gibbs* extends to new parties, not just new claims

The central question: Can a federal court exercise supplemental jurisdiction over additional parties when Congress has not expressly authorized it?

This is where the doctrine confronts the limits of its own lungs.

Internal Examination

Heart (Core Issue)

Does supplemental jurisdiction extend to pendent parties, or only to pendent claims?

Spine (Rule of Law)

The Court **tightens the spine**:

Federal courts may **not exercise pendent-party jurisdiction** unless Congress **expressly authorizes it.**

This is the opposite of *Gibbs.* It is a contraction — a vertebra snapping.

Brain (Reasoning)

This is where the doctrine becomes **restrictive, formalistic, and statute-bound.**

The Court reasons:

- Supplemental jurisdiction **is not constitutional; it is statutory**.
- The FTCA only authorizes suits against the United States, **not additional parties**.
- Courts cannot infer jurisdiction where **Congress has not**

granted it.

- *Gibbs* allowed **pendent claims, not pendent parties**.
- Expanding jurisdiction **without statutory authority violates separation of powers.**
- The judiciary **cannot enlarge its own jurisdiction**.

The brain becomes rigid: **No statutory authorization → no supplemental jurisdiction**.

Lungs (Tests Applied)

The doctrine struggles to breathe through:

- The distinction between pendent claims and pendent parties
- Strict statutory interpretation
- Limits on judicial power
- The absence of congressional authorization
- The need for explicit jurisdictional grants

These tests constrict the supplemental jurisdiction system.

Stomach (Facts Digested)

The Court digests:

- The FTCA's limited jurisdictional grant
- The lack of statutory language allowing suits against additional defendants
- The plaintiff's attempt to join city and utility defendants
- The factual relatedness (which *Gibbs* would have allowed)
- The statutory silence (which *Finley* treats as fatal)

These facts starve supplemental jurisdiction.

Cause of Death (for Pendent-Party Jurisdiction)

This case kills the idea that:

- Courts can add new parties under supplemental jurisdiction
- *Gibbs* extends to all related claims and parties
- Efficiency alone justifies jurisdiction
- Federal courts can infer jurisdiction from silence
- Supplemental jurisdiction is constitutionally self-executing

The doctrine becomes narrow, statutory, and suffocating.

Toxicology Report

External forces influencing the decision:

- Judicial caution about expanding federal power
- Strict textualism in the late 1980s
- Separation-of-powers concerns
- Fear of federal courts absorbing too many state-law disputes
- The rise of complex litigation without statutory guidance

These toxins shape the doctrine's metabolism.

Fractures and Weak Points

Even this rigid brain has fractures:

- The distinction between claims and parties is artificial
- The decision undermines judicial economy
- It contradicts the spirit of *Gibbs*
- It creates inefficiency and duplicative litigation
- It pressures Congress to intervene

These fractures will split open in § 1367.

Surviving Relatives

Finley strengthens:

- The principle that jurisdiction must be expressly granted
- The statutory nature of supplemental jurisdiction
- The limits of judicial power
- The need for congressional clarity

It becomes the doctrinal crisis that produces § 1367.

Future Prognosis

This case remains essential because it:

- Forces Congress to enact § 1367
- Defines the pre-statutory limits of supplemental jurisdiction
- Illustrates the dangers of statutory silence
- Shapes the modern understanding of pendent-party jurisdiction

It is the doctrine's collapse before rebirth.

Variable Manipulation

Changing one fact changes the outcome:

- If the FTCA expressly allowed suits against additional parties → jurisdiction
- If Congress had enacted § 1367 earlier → jurisdiction
- If the plaintiff sued the city and utility in state court → no federal issue

- If the federal claim were insubstantial → no supplemental jurisdiction at all

This teaches students how to diagnose statutory limits precisely.

Mini Lab

Suppose Congress had written the FTCA to allow suits against "the United States and any other responsible parties." Would *Finley* have come out differently?

Exxon Mobil Corp. v. Allapattah Services, Inc. (2005)

Full Legal Autopsy — Subject-Matter Jurisdiction (Supplemental Jurisdiction: Post-§1367 Expansion)

This is the cadaver that teaches the doctrine how to inhale entire classes of claims.

If *Gibbs* gave supplemental jurisdiction its lungs and *Finley* collapsed them, *Exxon Mobil v. Allapattah* is the case that restores full respiratory function under **28 U.S.C. § 1367**. This is the moment the doctrine learns how far § 1367(a) reaches — and how § 1367(b) limits that reach.

Identification of the Body

- **Case:** *Exxon Mobil Corp. v. Allapattah Services, Inc.*
- **Citation:** 545 U.S. 546 (2005)
- **Doctrine:** Subject-Matter Jurisdiction
- **Organ System:** Supplemental Jurisdiction (§ 1367)
- **Era:** Post-§1367 expansion

- **Reason for Autopsy:** This cadaver clarifies whether federal courts may exercise supplemental jurisdiction over **additional plaintiffs** who do not meet the amount-in-controversy requirement when at least one plaintiff does.

External Examination

The body presents with:

- A class action involving gas station dealers
- Some plaintiffs meeting the $75,000 amount-in-controversy requirement
- Other plaintiffs falling below the threshold
- A question about whether § 1367 allows these smaller claims to piggyback
- A need to interpret the interaction between § 1367(a) and § 1367(b)

The central question: **Can federal courts hear claims of additional plaintiffs who do not independently satisfy the amount-in-controversy requirement in diversity cases?**

This is where the doctrine confronts the scope of supplemental jurisdiction after Congress intervened.

Internal Examination

Heart (Core Issue)

Does § 1367 permit supplemental jurisdiction over **additional plaintiffs** whose claims fall below the jurisdictional amount when complete diversity exists?

Spine (Rule of Law)

The Court establishes:

When at least one plaintiff satisfies the amount-in-controversy requirement, § 1367(a) allows supplemental jurisdiction over additional plaintiffs whose claims do not — **as long as complete diversity is preserved**.

And:

§ 1367(b) restricts supplemental jurisdiction only in cases involving **claims by plaintiffs against persons made parties under Rules 14, 19, 20, or 24** — not claims by additional plaintiffs.

These vertebrae form the backbone of modern supplemental jurisdiction.

Brain (Reasoning)

This is where the doctrine develops its statutory intelligence.

The Court reasons:

- Congress enacted § 1367 to **overrule Finley** and restore broad supplemental jurisdiction.
- § 1367(a) is a **broad grant** of jurisdiction.
- § 1367(b) is a **narrow exception** that does not apply to additional plaintiffs.
- The statute's text controls — not policy concerns.
- The amount-in-controversy requirement applies only to the claims of plaintiffs who invoke original jurisdiction.
- Once one plaintiff satisfies § 1332, the others may join under § 1367(a).

The brain becomes clear: **§ 1367 is a statute of inclusion, not exclusion.**

Lungs (Tests Applied)

The doctrine breathes through:

- § 1367(a)'s broad grant

- § 1367(b)'s narrow exceptions
- Complete diversity requirement
- The time-of-filing rule
- The principle that supplemental jurisdiction extends to additional plaintiffs
- The need for statutory fidelity

These tests oxygenate the modern supplemental jurisdiction system.

Stomach (Facts Digested)

The Court digests:

- One plaintiff met the amount-in-controversy requirement
- Other plaintiffs did not
- All plaintiffs were diverse from the defendant
- The claims arose from the same nucleus of operative fact
- § 1367(a) applied
- § 1367(b) did not bar jurisdiction

These facts nourish supplemental jurisdiction.

Cause of Death (for the Strict Amount-in-Controversy Theory)

This case kills the idea that:

- Every plaintiff must independently meet the amount-in-controversy requirement
- Supplemental jurisdiction cannot apply to additional plaintiffs
- § 1367 is narrow
- *Finley* still limits modern supplemental jurisdiction
- Diversity cases must exclude small claims

The doctrine becomes expansive, statutory, and inclusive.

Toxicology Report

External forces influencing the decision:

- Congressional intent to overrule *Finley*
- The rise of class actions and mass litigation
- The need for efficiency
- The desire to avoid duplicative state and federal suits
- The importance of textualism in the early 2000s

These toxins shape the doctrine's metabolism.

Fractures and Weak Points

Even this brain has fractures:

- Does § 1367 apply to defendants' claims?
- How to treat minimal diversity class actions under CAFA?
- What about claims that dominate the litigation?
- How to treat jurisdictional manipulation?
- What about plaintiffs added after filing?

These fractures will later split open in lower-court interpretations.

Surviving Relatives

Allapattah strengthens:

- § 1367(a)'s broad reach
- The modern understanding of supplemental jurisdiction
- The distinction between claims and parties
- The principle that complete diversity is the only diversity

requirement

- The efficiency goals of federal jurisdiction

It becomes the doctrinal parent of all modern supplemental jurisdiction cases.

Future Prognosis

This case remains essential because it:

- Defines the scope of supplemental jurisdiction
- Clarifies the meaning of § 1367
- Shapes class action and multi-plaintiff litigation
- Anchors modern diversity practice
- Restores the lungs collapsed in *Finley*

It is the doctrine's **full lung capacity**.

Variable Manipulation

Changing one fact changes the outcome:

- If complete diversity were destroyed → no jurisdiction
- If the lead plaintiff did not meet the amount → no jurisdiction
- If plaintiffs sued additional defendants under Rule 20 → § 1367(b) might bar
- If the claims were unrelated → no supplemental jurisdiction

This teaches students how to diagnose § 1367 precisely.

Mini Lab

Suppose the lead plaintiff meets the amount-in-controversy requirement, but a second plaintiff sues an additional defendant under Rule 20. Does § 1367(b) bar supplemental

jurisdiction?

V. Removal Jurisdiction

Shamrock Oil & Gas Corp. v. Sheets (1941)

Full Legal Autopsy — Subject-Matter Jurisdiction (Removal: Who May Remove)

This is the cadaver that teaches the doctrine who is allowed to carry a case across the federal threshold.

If *Caterpillar* taught the doctrine when removal defects can be cured, *Shamrock Oil* teaches the doctrine the first rule of removal: Only defendants may remove — never plaintiffs.

This is the case that gives removal its entry gate.

Identification of the Body

- **Case:** *Shamrock Oil & Gas Corp. v. Sheets*
- **Citation:** 313 U.S. 100 (1941)
- **Doctrine:** Subject-Matter Jurisdiction
- **Organ System:** Removal (§ 1441)
- **Era:** Foundational limitation
- **Reason for Autopsy:** This cadaver establishes that plaintiffs may not remove, even if they become counterclaim defendants. It is the doctrine's first boundary line.

External Examination

The body presents with:

- Shamrock Oil filing a breach-of-contract action in state court
- The defendant filing a counterclaim against Shamrock
- Shamrock attempting to remove the case to federal court
- A question about whether a plaintiff-turned-counterclaim-defendant counts as a

"defendant" under the removal statute

- A need to interpret the meaning of "defendant" in § 1441

The central question: **Can a plaintiff remove a case to federal court after being hit with a counterclaim?**

This is where the doctrine confronts the identity of the "defendant."

Internal Examination

Heart (Core Issue)

Does the term **"defendant"** in the removal statute **include a plaintiff who becomes a counterclaim defendant?**

Spine (Rule of Law)

The Court establishes **a strict rule:**

Only the **original defendant** may remove **a case to federal court. A plaintiff may never remove — not even when facing a counterclaim.**

This spine supports all modern removal doctrine.

Brain (Reasoning)

This is where the doctrine develops its linguistic and structural intelligence.

The Court reasons:

- The removal statute must be strictly construed.
- Congress used the word "defendant" intentionally.
- A plaintiff chooses the forum and cannot later escape it.
- Allowing plaintiffs to remove would undermine the structure of removal.
- Counterclaims do not transform plaintiffs into defendants for removal purposes.

- The statute's history shows Congress intended a narrow removal right.

The brain becomes clear: Removal is a defendant's privilege — never a plaintiff's escape hatch.

Lungs (Tests Applied)

The doctrine breathes through:

- Strict construction of removal statutes
- The original-defendant rule
- The plaintiff-forum-choice principle
- The structural integrity of § 1441
- The need to prevent forum manipulation

These tests oxygenate the removal system.

Stomach (Facts Digested)

The Court digests:

- Shamrock Oil voluntarily chose state court
- The defendant counterclaimed
- Shamrock attempted to remove as a counterclaim defendant
- The statute did not authorize such removal
- Congress intended removal to be narrow

These facts starve removal jurisdiction.

Cause of Death (for Plaintiff-Removal Theory)

This case kills the idea that:

- Plaintiffs can remove their own cases
- Counterclaims transform plaintiffs into defendants

- Removal is a general right
- Removal statutes should be interpreted broadly
- Plaintiffs can escape their chosen forum

The doctrine becomes strict, narrow, and text-bound.

Toxicology Report

External forces influencing the decision:

- Historical suspicion of federal-court expansion
- The need to protect state-court authority
- Congressional intent to limit removal
- Fear of plaintiffs gaming the system
- The structural logic of adversarial litigation

These toxins shape the doctrine's metabolism.

Fractures and Weak Points

Even this strict brain has fractures:

- What about third-party defendants?
- What about removal under special statutes (e.g., CAFA)?
- What about federal-officer removal?
- What about bankruptcy-related removal?
- How to treat realignment of parties?

These fractures will later split open in cases like *Home Depot v. Jackson* (2019).

Surviving Relatives

Shamrock Oil strengthens:

- The original-defendant rule
- Strict construction of removal statutes
- The plaintiff's forum-choice principle
- The structural limits of § 1441
- The modern understanding of removal jurisdiction

It becomes the doctrinal ancestor of all removal-eligibility cases.

Future Prognosis

This case remains essential because it:

- Defines who may remove
- Prevents plaintiffs from manipulating jurisdiction
- Anchors the structure of removal practice
- Shapes modern statutory interpretation
- Protects the federal-state balance

It is the doctrine's removal gatekeeper.

Variable Manipulation

Changing one fact changes the outcome:

- If Shamrock had been sued originally → removal allowed
- If Congress amended § 1441 to include counterclaim defendants → removal allowed
- If the defendant filed a third-party claim → still no removal by the third-party defendant
- If the case involved federal-officer removal → special statute applies

This teaches students how to diagnose removal eligibility precisely.

Mini Lab

Suppose a defendant files a third-party complaint against a new party. Can that third-party defendant remove the case under *Shamrock Oil*?

Caterpillar Inc. v. Lewis (1996)

Full Legal Autopsy — Subject-Matter Jurisdiction (Removal & Cured Defects)

This is the cadaver that teaches the doctrine when a fatal jurisdictional wound can heal.

If *Mottley* taught the doctrine that SMJ is non-waivable, *Caterpillar* teaches the doctrine something more nuanced: **A removal defect does not kill a case if subject-matter jurisdiction exists at the time of judgment.**

This is the case that gives removal doctrine its **triage logic**.

Identification of the Body

- **Case:** *Caterpillar Inc. v. Lewis*
- **Citation:** 519 U.S. 61 (1996)
- **Doctrine:** Subject-Matter Jurisdiction
- **Organ System:** Removal & Remand (§§ 1441–1447)
- **Era:** Modern clarification of cured defects
- **Reason for Autopsy:** This cadaver teaches the doctrine when a premature removal is fatal — and when later events cure the defect.

External Examination

The body presents with:

- A state-court tort action
- Multiple defendants, including one non-diverse party
- Caterpillar removing the case to federal court **before** the non-diverse defendant was dismissed
- A jurisdictional defect at the moment of removal
- The non-diverse defendant being dismissed **before trial**
- A full federal trial and verdict
- A question about whether the entire case must be vacated due to improper removal

The central question: **Does a premature removal require vacating a judgment if complete diversity exists by the time of trial?**

This is where the doctrine confronts the difference between **removal defects** and **subject-matter jurisdiction**.

Internal Examination

Heart (Core Issue)

Is a removal defect fatal when **subject-matter jurisdiction exists at the time of judgment**?

Spine (Rule of Law)

The Court establishes:

A removal defect does not require vacating a judgment **if** the federal court had subject-matter jurisdiction at the time it entered judgment.

And:

Removal defects are **statutory**, not constitutional.

These vertebrae support modern removal doctrine.

Brain (Reasoning)

This is where the doctrine develops its emergency-room intelligence.

The Court reasons:

- Removal was improper because complete diversity did not exist at the time of removal.
- But the non-diverse defendant was dismissed before trial.
- By the time the case reached judgment, complete diversity existed.
- The federal court had **subject-matter jurisdiction** at the time of judgment.
- Vacating the judgment would waste judicial resources.
- The statutory removal defect did not undermine the court's constitutional power.

The brain becomes clear: **SMJ defects are fatal; removal defects are not — if cured in time.**

Lungs (Tests Applied)

The doctrine breathes through:

- The time-of-judgment rule
- The distinction between statutory and constitutional defects
- The complete diversity requirement
- Judicial economy
- Harmless-error principles
- The non-waivability of SMJ vs. waivability of removal defects

These tests oxygenate removal doctrine.

Stomach (Facts Digested)

The Court digests:

- Removal occurred prematurely
- The non-diverse defendant was dismissed before trial
- Complete diversity existed at judgment
- The federal court had constitutional power at the end
- No party was prejudiced
- A full federal trial had already occurred

These facts nourish the cured-defect doctrine.

Cause of Death (for the Strict Removal-Defect Theory)

This case kills the idea that:

- Any removal defect requires automatic remand
- Removal defects are jurisdictional
- Federal courts must vacate judgments due to early procedural errors
- Subject-matter jurisdiction must exist at the moment of removal
- Judicial economy is irrelevant to jurisdiction

The doctrine becomes pragmatic, flexible, and judgment-focused.

Toxicology Report

External forces influencing the decision:

- The rise of complex multi-party litigation
- The need to prevent wasteful retrials
- Judicial economy concerns
- The distinction between statutory and constitutional limits

- The desire to avoid gamesmanship

These toxins shape the doctrine's metabolism.

Fractures and Weak Points

Even this brain has fractures:

- What if the non-diverse defendant is dismissed after trial begins?
- What if the dismissal is strategic?
- What if the defect is more serious than premature removal?
- How to treat fraudulent joinder?
- What about cases removed without any plausible basis?

These fractures will later split open in lower-court removal jurisprudence.

Surviving Relatives

Caterpillar strengthens:

- The distinction between SMJ and removal defects
- The principle that SMJ must exist at judgment
- Judicial economy considerations
- The modern understanding of § 1447
- The flexibility of federal removal doctrine

It becomes the doctrinal parent of all "cured defect" cases.

Future Prognosis

This case remains essential because it:

- Defines when removal defects are fatal
- Clarifies the timing of jurisdictional analysis

- Prevents wasteful retrials
- Shapes modern removal practice
- Anchors the doctrine in pragmatic reasoning

It is the doctrine's **triage logic**.

Variable Manipulation

Changing one fact changes the outcome:

- If the non-diverse defendant remained at judgment → no jurisdiction
- If the dismissal occurred after judgment → defect not cured
- If the federal court lacked SMJ at judgment → fatal
- If the defect were constitutional → incurable

This teaches students how to diagnose removal defects precisely.

Mini Lab

Suppose the non-diverse defendant is dismissed *after* the jury returns a verdict but *before* the court enters judgment. Under *Caterpillar*, is the defect cured?

VI. The Final Anatomy

SYNTHESIS CHAPTER

The Living Body of Subject-Matter Jurisdiction

Subject-Matter Jurisdiction is not a list of statutes or a checklist of cases. It is a **living organism** — one that has expanded, contracted, fractured, healed, and reorganized itself over more than two centuries.

After dissecting each case under the scalpel, this chapter steps back from the operating table to examine the doctrine as a whole body.

This is where the pieces become a system.

The Evolutionary Anatomy of the Doctrine

1. The Genetic Code — Strawbridge v. Curtiss (1806)

The doctrine begins with the DNA of **complete diversity**. Every plaintiff must be diverse from every defendant. This genetic code still governs today.

2. The Cosmic Brain — Osborn v. Bank of the United States (1824)

Marshall gives Article III a vast, cosmic brain. Any federal ingredient is enough for constitutional jurisdiction. This is the **outer limit** of federal power.

3. The Skin — Mottley (1908)

The doctrine gains its surface layer: Federal jurisdiction must appear on the **face of the complaint**. Federal defenses do not count.

4. The Heartbeat — American Well Works (1916)

A case arises under the law that **creates the cause of action**. This becomes the default heartbeat of §1331.

5. The Triage System — Bell v. Hood (1946)

Jurisdiction and merits become separate organs. If the federal claim is not frivolous, the court has jurisdiction — even if the claim will lose.

6. The Gatekeeper — Shamrock Oil (1941)

Only defendants may remove. The doctrine gains its first doorway.

7. The Lungs — United Mine Workers v. Gibbs (1966)

Supplemental jurisdiction takes its first breath. Claims sharing a **common nucleus of operative fact** may be heard together.

8. The Collapse — Finley (1989)

The lungs collapse. No pendent-party jurisdiction without explicit statutory authorization.

9. The Revival — 28 U.S.C. §1367 (1990)

Congress revives the lungs with a statutory oxygen tank. Supplemental jurisdiction becomes codified.

10. The Expansion — Exxon Mobil v. Allapattah (2005)

§1367 allows additional plaintiffs who do not meet the amount-in-controversy requirement — as long as one plaintiff does.

11. The Cured Wound — Caterpillar Inc. v. Lewis (1996)

A premature removal does not kill a case if jurisdiction exists at judgment. The doctrine learns to distinguish **fatal** defects from **curable** ones.

12. The Frozen Body — Grupo Dataflux (2004)

Diversity is frozen at the moment of filing. Later changes cannot resurrect a dead case.

13. The Microscope — Grable (2005)

A state-law claim may arise under federal law if the embedded federal issue is:

- necessarily raised

- actually disputed
- substantial
- and jurisdiction does not disturb federal-state balance

The doctrine gains precision.

14. The Filter — Gunn v. Minton (2013)

The federal issue must be **substantial to the federal system**, not just the parties. The microscope gains a filter.

The Modern Body: How Subject-Matter Jurisdiction Works Today

Federal Question Jurisdiction (The Heart and Brain)

A case arises under federal law when:

1. The Heart — Creation Test (American Well Works)

The cause of action is created by federal law.

2. The Brain — Embedded Federal Issue (Grable/Gunn)

A state-law claim may arise under federal law if the federal issue is:

- necessarily raised
- actually disputed
- substantial to the federal system
- and jurisdiction is consistent with federal-state balance

3. The Skin — Mottley

The federal issue must appear on the face of the complaint.

4. The Triage — Bell v. Hood

If the federal claim is not frivolous, jurisdiction exists.

Diversity Jurisdiction (The Skeleton)

Diversity jurisdiction has a rigid skeletal structure:

1. Bones — Complete Diversity (Strawbridge)

No plaintiff may share citizenship with any defendant.

2. Bone Marrow — Citizenship Rules

- Individuals → domicile (Mas)
- Corporations → place of incorporation + nerve center (Hertz)
- Partnerships/LLCs → citizenship of every member (Grupo Dataflux)

3. Bone Density — Amount in Controversy (St. Paul Mercury)

The claim must exceed $75,000 unless it is legally impossible.

4. Frozen Bones — Time-of-Filing Rule (Grupo Dataflux)

Jurisdiction is determined at filing and cannot be cured by later changes.

Supplemental Jurisdiction (The Lungs)

Supplemental jurisdiction breathes through:

1. Common Nucleus (Gibbs)

Claims must arise from the same nucleus of operative fact.

2. Statutory Oxygen (28 U.S.C. §1367)

Codifies supplemental jurisdiction.

3. Additional Plaintiffs (Allapattah)

If one plaintiff meets the amount requirement, others may join.

4. Limits (1367(b))

Bars certain claims in diversity cases to prevent circumvention.

Removal Jurisdiction (The Gateways)

1. The Gatekeeper — Shamrock Oil

Only defendants may remove.

2. The Cured Wound — Caterpillar

Removal defects are curable if jurisdiction exists at judgment.

3. The Uncured Wound — Grupo Dataflux

Jurisdictional defects at filing are fatal.

Exam-Ready Flowchart

Flowchart 1 — The SMJ Master Algorithm

Step 1 — Identify the Basis of Jurisdiction

- Federal Question?
- Diversity?
- Supplemental?
- Removal?

If unclear → analyze all.

Flowchart 2 — Federal Question Jurisdiction (§1331)

Part 1 — Creation Test (American Well Works)

Does federal law create the cause of action?

- Yes → Jurisdiction exists.
- No → Move to embedded issue.

Part 2 — Embedded Federal Issue (Grable/Gunn)

Is the federal issue:

- necessarily raised
- actually disputed
- substantial to the federal system
- jurisdictionally appropriate?

If yes → Jurisdiction exists. If no → No §1331 jurisdiction.

Part 3 — Mottley Check

Is the federal issue on the face of the complaint? If no → No jurisdiction.

Part 4 — Bell v. Hood Check

Is the federal claim non-frivolous? If yes → Jurisdiction exists.

Flowchart 3 — Diversity Jurisdiction (§1332)

Part 1 — Complete Diversity (Strawbridge)

Is every P diverse from every D? If no → Jurisdiction fails.

Part 2 — Citizenship

- Individuals → domicile
- Corporations → incorporation + nerve center
- Partnerships/LLCs → all members

Part 3 — Amount in Controversy

Does the claim exceed $75,000? If legally impossible → fails.

Part 4 — Time-of-Filing Rule

Was diversity complete at filing? If not → fatal defect.

Flowchart 4 — Supplemental Jurisdiction (§1367)

Step 1 — Common Nucleus (Gibbs)

Do the claims arise from the same nucleus of operative fact?

Step 2 — Statutory Grant (§1367(a))

If yes → supplemental jurisdiction exists unless barred.

Step 3 — Statutory Limits (§1367(b))

In diversity cases, certain claims by plaintiffs are barred.

Step 4 — Discretion (Gibbs)

Even if allowed, the court may decline.

Flowchart 5 — Removal Jurisdiction (§1441)

Step 1 — Who May Remove?

Only defendants (Shamrock Oil).

Step 2 — Basis for Removal

- Federal question
- Diversity
- Special statutes

Step 3 — Defects

- Procedural defects → curable (Caterpillar)
- Jurisdictional defects → fatal (Grupo Dataflux)

Flowchart 6 — Quick Reference Case Map

- **Complete Diversity** → Strawbridge
- **Constitutional Federal Ingredient** → Osborn
- **Well-Pleaded Complaint** → Mottley
- **Creation Test** → American Well Works
- **Non-Frivolous Claim** → Bell v. Hood
- **Only Defendants May Remove** → Shamrock Oil
- **Common Nucleus** → Gibbs
- **No Pendent-Party Jurisdiction** → Finley
- **Supplemental Jurisdiction Expanded** → Allapattah
- **Cured Removal Defects** → Caterpillar
- **Time-of-Filing Rule** → Grupo Dataflux
- **Embedded Federal Issue** → Grable
- **Substantiality Filter** → Gunn

Glossary of Anatomical Terms

Law Under the Scalpel: Case Dissections

This glossary explains the anatomical metaphors used throughout this series. Each term represents a specific function in the dissection of a case — helping readers see doctrine not as scattered rules, but as a living body with structure, purpose, and evolution.

The Heart

The emotional and doctrinal core of the case — the central question or principle that keeps the doctrine alive. This is the "why it matters."

The Spine

The rule of law that supports the entire case. The spine is the structural backbone: strong, clear, and essential for doctrinal stability.

The Brain

The Court's reasoning — the intellectual engine that explains *how* the rule was formed. This is where logic, policy, and interpretation converge.

The Lungs

The doctrinal tests or standards that allow the rule to "breathe" across different fact patterns. The lungs show how the case functions in real-world application.

The Stomach

The essential facts digested down to their functional core. Only what truly feeds the rule survives this cut.

The Skin

The holding — the outward, final layer of the case. It is what the doctrine looks like once the reasoning and facts are fully assembled.

The Muscles

The practical strength of the case — how it moves doctrine, shapes future decisions, or empowers litigants. (Used in some dissections where the case adds force or flexibility.)

The Bones

The foundational principles or historical structures that support the doctrine. These are the oldest, most rigid elements of the legal body.

The Marrow

The deeper policy values or constitutional principles that nourish the doctrine from within.

The Fractures

Weaknesses, tensions, or unresolved conflicts within the case. These are the cracks that later cases may widen or repair.

The Toxicology Report

External influences — political, historical, or social — that shaped the Court's decision. This reveals what was in the bloodstream of the era.

The Cause of Death

What the case overrules, replaces, or renders obsolete. This shows how doctrine evolves through loss and renewal.

The Future Prognosis

The case's legacy — how it will influence doctrine moving forward. This is the long-term health forecast.

Variable Manipulation

A brief exploration of how small factual changes alter the outcome. This teaches readers how to think like lawyers, not just memorize rules.

Mini-Lab

A short, exam-ready hypothetical that allows readers to test the rule immediately. This is hands-on doctrinal practice.

Case Index

Subject-Matter Jurisdiction — Law Under the Scalpel: Case Dissections

- **Shamrock Oil & Gas Corp. v. Sheets (1941)** — Only Defendants May Remove
- **St. Paul Mercury Indemnity Co. v. Red Cab Co. (1938)** — Amount in Controversy
- **Strawbridge v. Curtiss (1806)** — Complete Diversity

About the Author

Anjanette G. Seymour is a law tutor, compliance professional, and the visionary creator of the *Law in Pieces* series — a collection of narrative-driven study snippets designed to make complex doctrine clear, memorable, and human. She holds an LL.M. from the University of Maryland Francis King Carey School of Law and an LL.B. (Hons.) from the University of London, along with certification as a Risk and Compliance Management Professional (CRCMP).

Her path to law began in the world of banking, where the aftermath of September 11th and the sweeping transformation of financial regulations ignited her desire to understand — and help others understand — the evolving landscape of legal oversight and financial crime prevention. When her position was made redundant, she embraced the opportunity to deepen her studies, ultimately shaping a career grounded in clarity, integrity, and service.

Today, Anjanette is a self-published author and dedicated law tutor whose passion lies in transforming doctrine into stories students can actually *feel* and remember. Through her signature "Under the Scalpel" method — dissecting cases into their heart, spine, brain, lungs, stomach, and fractures — she brings the law to life as a living body with structure, purpose, and evolution.

Her work blends precision with creativity, offering readers not just rules, but understanding; not just summaries, but insight; not just study aids, but epiphany. The *Law in Pieces* series reflects her belief that every student deserves clarity, confidence, and a way into the law that feels human.

When she is not writing or tutoring, Anjanette continues to expand her creative world through art, design, and storytelling — always building, always imagining, always empowering others to see the beauty in both the law and themselves.

www.ingramcontent.com/pod-product-compliance
Lightning Source LLC
LaVergne TN
LVHW022230200926
848481LV00006B/2200
* 9 7 9 8 9 9 5 8 9 2 3 3 5 *